Solving the Part-Time Puzzle:

The Law Firm's Guide to Balanced Hours

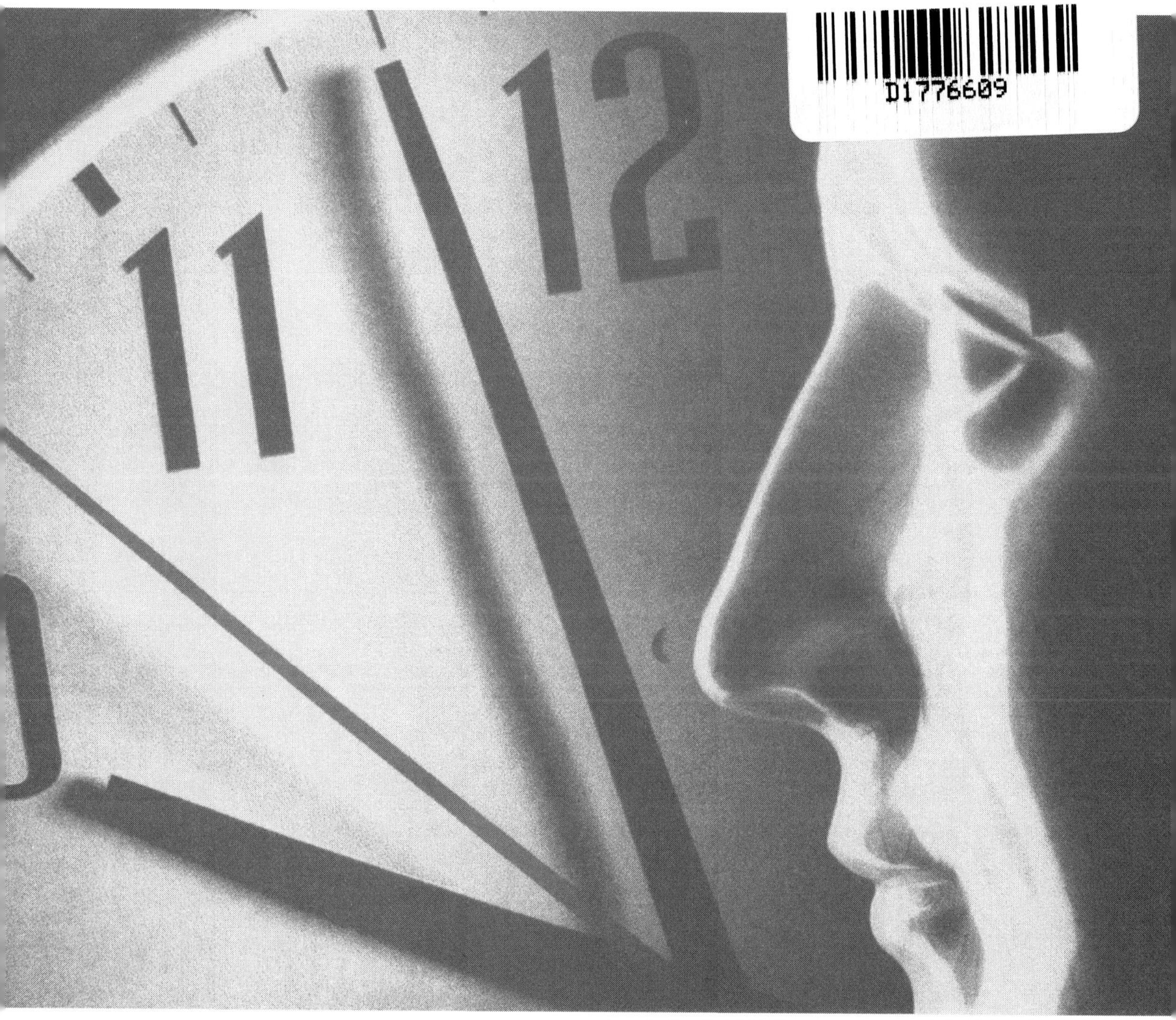

by Joan C. Williams and Cynthia Thomas Calvert

NALP

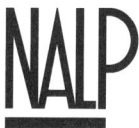

Dedication

To Walter, Kate and Sarah, the "life" in my work/life balance. — CTC
To Ruth and Xavier Dempsey. — JCW

© 2004 National Association for Law Placement, Inc.®
All rights reserved.

The PAR Usability Test is reprinted with permission and is copyrighted (© 2001) by Joan Williams. All rights reserved.

The Attrition Cost Worksheet presented as Appendix 3 is reprinted with permission and is copyrighted (© 2003) by Cynthia Thomas Calvert. All rights reserved.

The Model Balanced Hours Policy presented as Appendix 5 is reprinted with permission and is copyrighted (© 2001) by Joan Williams and Cynthia Thomas Calvert. All rights reserved.

ISBN 1-55733-042-5

1025 Connecticut Avenue NW, Suite 1110
Washington, DC 20036-5413
(202) 835-1001 — Fax (202) 835-1112 — info@nalp.org
www.nalp.org
Additional sites: www.nalpdirectory.com — www.pslawnet.org — www.nalpfoundation.org

Contents

Foreword by James J. Sandman, *Managing Partner, Arnold & Porter LLP* 7

Part One: The Foundations of Balanced Hours Programs 9

Chapter 1: Profitability from Balanced Hours Programs 11
    Why Do Firms Need Balanced Hours Programs? 11
    The Demand for Fewer Hours 12
    Which Attorneys Want to Work Fewer Hours? 12
    Time Over Money...13
        Sidebar: Who Leaves Law Firms? 14
    Benefits to Firms 15
        Sidebar: One Firm's Experience 20
        Sidebar: Sample Award Winners 21
        Case Studies: Can Firms Really Save Money with Balanced Hours Programs? 22
    Chapter Summary 23

Chapter 2: How Current Part-Time Programs Hurt Law Firms 25
    The Problems..25
        Sidebar: Schedule Creep Scenarios 27
        Sidebar: Real-Life Stigma 30
    The Communication Gap..31
    The PAR Usability Test 31
        Sidebar: The PAR Usability Test..31
        Sidebar: Comparison of Two Firms' Part-Time Programs 33
        Sidebar: Sample Calculation of Median Schedules and Durations 34
        Sidebar: Examples of Measuring Schedule Creep 35
    So How Are Balanced Hours Programs Different? 37
    Chapter Summary 39

Chapter 3: The Myth of Unprofitability **41**

    Fallacy #1: High Lawyer Productivity Is the Only Path to
Firm Profitability 41

    Fallacy #2: Lawyers Are Fungible Billing Machines for Whom an
Hour in the Office Is an Hour Billed 42

        Sidebar: Full-time Hours Don't Mean Full-time Billing 43

    Fallacy #3: Part-time Lawyers Generate Less Revenue Than Their Overhead ... 44

        Sidebar: Why Is Overhead Even an Issue? 44

        Sidebar: Excess Costs? 45

    Overhead vs. Personnel 46

    The Bottom Line.. 47

    Chapter Summary 48

Part Two: Creating and Implementing Balanced Hours Programs **49**

Chapter 4: Laying the Foundation for a Balanced Hours Program **51**

    Initial Considerations... 52

        Sidebar: Some Data to Gather 53

    Build the Foundation 53

        Sidebar: Tips for Identifying Key Players 54

        Sidebar: Conversation Starters 55

        Sidebar: Suggested Talking Points for Key Player Conversations 56

        Sidebar: Excerpt from a Sample Plan 59

    Chapter Summary 60

Chapter 5: Assessing the Firm's Needs **61**

    Quantitative Assessments 61

        Sidebar: Dickstein, Shapiro 62

    PAR Usability Test 65

    Qualitative Assessment.. 65

        Sidebar: What Is Being Said 69

    Chapter Summary 70

Chapter 6: Creating a Balanced Hours Policy **71**

    Process... 71

    Fundamental Principles 71

Why Have a Written Policy? 72
Essential Elements of a Balanced Hours Program 73
    Sidebar: Troubleshooting Schedule Creep 83
    Sidebar: Tips for Conducting Reviews 85
Additional Considerations 86
Chapter Summary 90

Chapter 7: Implementing the Policy 91
Leadership 91
    Sidebar: One Managing Partner's Commitment 92
    Sidebar: Leadership Action Points 93
Communication 94
    Sidebar: Sample Agenda for Group Meetings 96
    Sidebar: How to Encourage Discussion 97
Training 98
    Sidebar: Examples of Unexamined Biases 103
    Sidebar: Deloitte's Training Program 104
    Sidebar: Leveraging Experience at Ernst & Young 105
Assessment 106
Chapter Summary 107

Chapter 8: Making the Program Work on a Firm Level 109
Appointing a Balanced Hours Coordinator 109
    Sidebar: Functions of a Balanced Hours Coordinator 110
Backlash Prevention 110
Balanced Hours Information Database 111
    Sidebar: A Database Example 112
Hold Partners Accountable 112
Performance Evaluations 113
Eliminate Myths about Commitment 114
Celebrate Successes 115
Coaching 115
    Sidebar: Coaching Is Good for Business 117
Fill the Firm with Supporters 117
Chapter Summary 118

Chapter 9: Making the Policy Work on an Individual Level 121
    Creating an Appropriate Schedule 121
    Support Groups and Mentors 122
    Providing Feedback 124
        Sidebar: Feedback Examples 124
    Maximizing Effectiveness 125
    Communicating with Supervisors and Clients 125
    Ensuring Professional and Business Development 127
        Sidebar: Suggestions for Encouraging Professional and
        *   Business Development* 127
    Chapter Summary 128

Chapter 10: Common Myths and Frequently Asked Questions 129
        Sidebar: Client Reactions to Balanced Hours 132

Appendices 143
    Appendix 1: Sample Memo to Firm Regarding New Policy 145
    Appendix 2: Sample Questionnaire 147
    Appendix 3: Attrition Cost Worksheet 151
    Appendix 4: Balanced Hours Schedule Checklist for Attorneys 157
    Appendix 5: Model Balanced Hours Policy 161

About the Authors 167
About NALP 168

Foreword

This is an important book.

Surveys have for years documented the unusually high levels of career dissatisfaction among lawyers. There are a number of reasons for this, but from everything I have seen — not only in surveys but in the scores of exit interviews I have conducted over nine years as Managing Partner of a large law firm — the single biggest source of dissatisfaction in our profession is the inability to achieve work/life balance. And the cause of that inability is the hours lawyers feel they are expected to work.

The inability to achieve work/life balance affects men as well as women. It has profound effects on the legal profession. It is the cause of significant attrition in law firms, with consequent disruptions in client service. It is the reason some lawyers leave altogether a career they entered with the noblest of goals — to make a difference in our society — without having realized their potential.

This book can and will make a difference. In *Solving the Part-Time Puzzle: The Law Firm's Guide to Balanced Hours,* Joan Williams and Cynthia Thomas Calvert demonstrate why they are the nation's leaders on balanced hours in the legal profession. Their leadership springs from their starting point: a clear-eyed recognition of the business needs of law firms and the service requirements of clients. That perspective pervades every aspect of their approach to the work/life balance challenge.

This book's greatest value lies in its pragmatism. Joan and Cynthia start by making the business case for balanced hours. Based on their usual meticulous and even-handed research, they identify the pitfalls of poorly planned part-time programs. They debunk the myths that have impeded the acceptance of effective balanced hours policies in law firms. They provide helpful, business-savvy advice on how to create and implement a successful balanced hours program, illustrated with real-world examples and best practices from a number of successful law firms. And they look beyond law firms, to other types of professional services organizations, for business lessons that are relevant and transferable.

The issue this book addresses is one in which I have great personal and professional interest. Reading it has given me new ideas and renewed passion in my conviction that effective balanced hours programs are in the best business interests of law firms and their clients.

James J. Sandman
Managing Partner
Arnold & Porter LLP

Part One:

The Foundations of Balanced Hours Programs

Chapter 1

Profitability from Balanced Hours Programs

Prominent, successful law firms have discovered that the new operating paradigm of balanced hours creates satisfied clients, attracts new business, and draws the best recruits like a magnet. These firms have capitalized on the changes in today's workforce, both inside law firms and in corporate clients' offices, and are profiting from stable client relationships and committed employees. Far from wondering if they will still be viable in five or ten years, they have taken steps to ensure their financial futures.

So, what are balanced hours programs? Balanced hours programs are work style programs that allow attorneys to reduce the number of hours they work without sacrificing their professional futures. As is explained in this book, balanced hours programs differ from traditional part-time programs in that law firms' business needs drive balanced hours programs, attorneys who reduce their hours are not stigmatized, and workloads are actively managed to ensure success.

■ Why Do Firms Need Balanced Hours Programs?

Law firms are on a treadmill of recruiting, training, developing, and losing lawyers. Too often, these are "regretted losses" — not hiring mistakes or fungible drones, but promising young attorneys with go-getter attitudes, strong skills, and rainmaking potential. Client relationships are eroded by the turnover, not only because of lost personal relationships, but also because of the aggravation and repetitive costs of bringing new attorneys up to speed. Within firms, lost personal relationships — or the inability to develop relationships in the first place — hurt morale. Bottom lines suffer as partners' attention is diverted from client service and as firms spend millions of dollars each year in out-of-pocket recruiting and retraining expenses and administrative costs.

■ The Demand for Fewer Hours

Law firm billable hour requirements have increased dramatically over the past 40 years. What was considered full-time law practice in 1961 — about 25 hours per week[1] — would be considered very part-time by today's standards. Many attorneys either cannot or will not work 60 or more hours per week on a regular basis. Time demands from families or outside interests, physical stamina, or mental health make working long hours not an option. Studies show a strong correlation between the rise in billable hour requirements in private law practice and lawyer dissatisfaction, depression, and burnout.[2]

■ Which Attorneys Want to Work Fewer Hours?

Mention "part-time" work and a picture springs to mind of a woman attorney with young children trying to juggle her work and family obligations. Indeed, mothers often find high billable hour requirements hard to meet while they bear the bulk of the responsibility for caregiving; they are pulled in one direction by societal agreement that young children should be raised by their parents and in another by law firms that expect attorneys to work 60 hours per week or more. However, while mothers of young children were the first to be vocal about the need for fewer hours, others are now also demanding more time to take care of personal obligations:

- *Fathers.* Increasingly, men want to work fewer hours in order to care for their children. A Catalyst study of the graduates of six elite law schools found that 71% of law graduates with children — both men and women — report work/life conflict.[3] Another study found that slightly over 70% of men in their twenties and thirties said that they would be willing to take lower salaries in exchange for more family time.[4]

---

[1] An Oregon State Bar survey conducted in 1961 showed that lawyers nationwide billed an average of 1,236 hours annually. Reported on http://www.emplawyernet.com/courts.

[2] Boston Bar Association Task Force on Work-Life Balance, "Facing The Grail: Confronting the Cost of Work-Family Imbalance," June 1999; American Bar Association report, "At the Breaking Point: A National Conference on the Emerging Crisis in the Quality of Lawyers' Health and Lives — Its Impact on Law Firms and Client Services," 1991. See Patrick J. Schiltz, "On Being a Happy, Healthy and Ethical Member of an Unhappy, Unhealthy and Unethical Profession," *Vanderbilt Law Review*, vol. 52, no. 4, May 1999.

[3] Catalyst, *Women in Law: Making the Case* (Catalyst, 2001) at 18.

[4] Kirstin Downey Grimsley, "Family a Priority for Young Workers; Survey Finds Change in Men's Thinking," *The Washington Post*, May 3, 2000 at E1.

- *Non-parents.* The high billable hour requirement of most law firms has made it all but impossible for attorneys to pursue interests outside of the office. Attorneys who want to teach, run marathons, write, or travel want to work fewer hours. In addition, more and more attorneys are finding a need to cut back in order to care for elderly parents or sick partners.[5]

- *Gen-Xers.* Studies show that Generation Xers — males as well as females — are much less willing than baby boomers to "give their all" to their employer. Many saw their fathers give up everything for companies that later fired them. Compared to today's baby-boom partners, male Gen-Xers are less likely to be men married to stay-at-home wives or to women who work part-time and take care of virtually all household matters. And some Gen-Xers also have obligations as caretakers, either of children or others.

When attorneys cannot find the time they need in their busy law firm schedules, and when part-time work is not available to them or is discouraged, they leave their firms. Notably, few tell their firms that they are leaving for reasons related to scheduling, and men tend to be less forthcoming than women. Rather, they often say they are leaving to pursue another opportunity or because they have always wanted to teach, or cite similar factors. They don't want to risk burning any bridges or damaging their reputation as valuable workers. The truth is revealed, however, in confidential interviews, anonymous surveys, and private conversations.

■ Time Over Money

If high hours drive attorneys away from their firms, it follows that increasing attorneys' salaries and requiring them to work longer hours to justify the increase will not convince them to stay. An American Management Association survey of 352 companies found that employers reported more success in retaining employees by "giving them a life" than by offering more cash.[6] A national survey of associates in large law firms found large percentages who would like to work fewer hours in exchange for less pay; these included Chicago's Wildman, Harrold, Allen & Dixon (72.2%), Boston's Hale and Dorr (67.7%), and Clifford Chance (65.6%).[7]

---

[5] The Women's Bureau of the U. S. Department of Labor has reported that almost one in four American households provides care to an elderly relative or friend, which impacts work schedules. *Work and Elder Care: Facts for Caregivers and Their Employers,* U.S. Department of Labor (1998).

[6] Sue Shellenbarger, "Employees Who Value Time as Much as Money Now Get Their Reward," *Wall Street Journal*, Sept. 22, 1999, at B1.

[7] 2002 Associates Survey, American Lawyer Media, October 1, 2002 (available at www.law.com).

Who Leaves Law Firms?

Each of the following is a composite based on true stories.

- **A male associate at a mid-sized law firm** had great credentials — top law school, law review, prestigious federal clerkship. He and his wife, a lawyer with similarly terrific credentials, decided to have a baby. Both wanted to be actively involved in raising the baby, and both wanted a good quality of life, but the firm would not allow flexibility. He left the law firm, and he and his wife became law professors.

- **A junior partner** had worked part-time for several years while an associate in order to raise her small children. Although she had returned to full-time, her status at the firm had clearly suffered. She received less money and less interesting work than her colleagues and was not selected to serve on firm committees. Anticipating further erosion in her professional status at the firm, she left to work for a nonprofit group.

- **A senior associate at a large law firm** that was frequently praised for being "family friendly" negotiated a part-time schedule while her children were young. Her agreement with the firm called for her to work 70% of a full-time schedule. Nevertheless, she was consistently having to work 60 or more hours per week. She was exhausted from trying to meet the conflicting demands of her office work and her life at home. Bringing home stacks of documents to review, traveling to meet with clients, and drafting emergency briefs late into the night left her with no time to see her children and filled her with stress. She left the firm to work in a corporate legal department.

- **An associate at a large, prestigious firm** worked typical firm hours and regularly billed in excess of 55 hours per week. He was in his office about 12 hours a day Monday through Friday and then worked another ten hours on the weekend. His work was good, clients liked him, and he was gaining prominence in the bar association. He enjoyed a salary higher than that of a Supreme Court Justice and many firm perks. When an opportunity came along for him to leave the legal profession for a job with much shorter hours, he jumped on it despite the corresponding and significant income reduction. He stated unequivocally that the hours drove him away.

Firms can give their attorneys a life in a number of ways: reduced hours, regular telecommuting, flexible scheduling, and job sharing are a few examples. Of these, reduced hours and telecommuting are the most sought after. While many firms offer these options, either formally or informally, typically they do not encourage them. In fact, as discussed in the next chapter, the use of part-time programs frequently is so stigmatized that it is not considered to be a real option by most attorneys. Given the bad reputation of part-time programs, and the dearth of information about successful part-time programs, this book focuses on part-time work.

■ Benefits to Firms

Balanced hours make good business sense, as a number of prominent and successful law firms have discovered. Among the firms that have implemented or are in the process of implementing non-stigmatized reduced-hours programs:

- Alston & Bird LLP
- Arnold & Porter LLP
- Davis Wright Tremaine LLP
- Debevoise & Plimpton
- Dickstein Shapiro Morin & Oshinsky LLP
- Goodwin Procter LLP
- Heller Ehrman White & McAuliffe LLP
- Morrison & Foerster LLP
- Pillsbury Winthrop LLP
- Piper Rudnick LLP
- Shearman & Sterling
- Vinson & Elkins LLP

Retention

Increased retention of the best and the brightest is the clearest benefit of balanced hours programs. Legal talent is a law firm's inventory. Recent studies of the causes of attrition show that a desire for work/life balance plays a significant role in associate departures.[8] Talented attorneys want fewer hours, but by and large they are not willing to

---

[8] *Keeping the Keepers II: Mobility & Management of Associates*, The NALP Foundation for Law Career Research & Education (2003), at 98; *Beyond the Bidding Wars: A Survey of Associate Attrition, Departure Destinations & Workplace Incentives*, The NALP Foundation for Law Career Research & Education (2000), at 17; Women's Bar Association of Massachusetts, *More Than Part Time: The Effect of Reduced-Hours Arrangements on the Retention, Recruitment, and Success of Women Attorneys in Law Firms* (2000); *Keeping the Keepers: Strategies for Associate Retention in Times of Attrition*, The NALP Foundation for Law Career Research & Education (1998).

sacrifice the professional success they have worked so long to achieve by reducing the number of hours they work. If they can't say this directly, they will speak with their feet.

Recruiting

Effective balanced hours programs make recruiting good attorneys substantially easier. Highly qualified applicants want to work for firms with good quality reduced-hours programs, either because they want to work part-time now or in the future, or because they just want to be at a firm that has a people-first attitude. Without a doubt, the availability of part-time work is a big draw. Catalyst found that work/life balance was the number one consideration for 45% of women law graduates in choosing their current employer.[9] Confirming this finding, PAR has received requests for lists of firms that have good programs from many law students and attorneys. PAR maintains a database on its web site, www.pardc.org, that provides information about the quality of balanced hours programs in firms in Washington, D.C. Bar associations and law school career services offices are considering putting similar information online about firms in other cities.

Improved Client Relationships

Perhaps the most important reason to improve retention through balanced hours is the most overlooked: the discontent of clients caused by constant turnover in the attorneys who represent them. Clients spend a lot of time and effort establishing working relationships with outside counsel, and they report that they are upset by high attrition.[10] Not only do they have to break in new attorneys, and perhaps even pay for a new attorney to get up to speed on a case, but they lose the momentum and the institutional memory of the departing attorney. Reducing attrition shows recognition of clients' needs and demonstrates the stability and quality of the firm.

---

[9] Catalyst, supra, n. 3.

[10] *Better on Balance? The Corporate Counsel Work/Life Report*, Project for Attorney Retention Corporate Counsel Project, December 2003 (available at www.pardc.org). The Corporate Counsel Project studied both work/life balance in corporate law departments and ways in which corporate counsel, as clients, can assist law firms in implementing balanced hours programs. Interviews with general counsels and their subordinates have included frequent and frank complaints about turnover at law firms.

> "Firms losing associates is a big issue for us and, honestly, it has caused us to move away from certain firms. I have expressed concerns when teams [in law firms] with institutional knowledge about our business fall apart because of departures. The burden of educating new attorneys is aggravating, and turning new associates loose on business clients can be a recipe for disaster."
>
> — A corporate counsel

Improved Business Development

A good balanced hours program that cuts attrition can help get new clients in several ways. First, PAR has heard reports of clients who are starting to consider a firm's attrition rate and average billable hours when deciding whether to hire them. A firm that can boast about its low turnover will have a clear leg up in a beauty contest. For example, Linda Madrid, general counsel at CarrAmerica, considers the quality of life at a law firm when deciding whether to hire the firm:

> "It is frustrating when outside counsel don't provide consistent lawyers.... [N]othing [is] worse than investing in and relying on someone, and then having that person pulled out. Or, even worse, the firm isn't treating them well enough to keep them. We have tried to look at how our outside counsel treat their young lawyers...including demands in terms of billing. These are all issues that we think ultimately have an impact on the services we receive."
>
> — Linda Madrid, General Counsel, CarrAmerica[11]

Second, clients want to hire law firms with values similar to their own so they can find common ground and forge bonds. They want to hire firms that, like themselves, have taken practical business steps to cut attrition, such as implementing work/life programs. Moreover, corporations are increasingly interested in implementing diversity initiatives through their buying power; firms that retain and promote women attorneys and attorneys of color will gain a competitive edge in the contest for new business.[12]

---

[11] Cynthia Thomas Calvert, "Focus on Doing Well, and the Opportunities Will Find You: A Profile of Linda Madrid," *Raising The Bar* (Women's Bar Association of the District of Columbia, Spring 2000), at 11.

[12] See, e.g., Nathan Koppel, "Shell's Reward for Diversity: Work," *The American Lawyer*, June 2004; Dr. Arin Reeves, "Diversity in Dollars and Sense," *Diversity & The Bar* (Minority Corporate Counsel Association), November 2002, available at http://www.mcca.com/site/data/magazine/coverstory/CEO1102.htm.

Some firms, such as Vinson & Elkins LLP and Wolf, Block, Schorr and Solis-Cohen LLP, are already viewing flexible work arrangements as a key ingredient in programs designed to attract and retain women and minorities to meet these client demands.[13]

Some corporations that require diversity in their outside counsel are:
- DuPont
- Bell South
- J.P. Morgan Chase & Co.
- Shell Oil Company
- Johnson & Johnson
- Bank of America

High attrition impacts client development in another very important way. The attorneys who leave law firms may be moving to corporate counsel positions where they will be potential clients. Are they going to hire a law firm they feel treated them badly or one they know has the ability to offer balance and retain its lawyers? It deserves a firm to have a large number of disgruntled former employees, regardless of where they are next employed. Word spreads quickly these days not only by word of mouth and e-mail but also via Internet bulletin boards and web sites devoted to tracking issues at law firms. A reputation for unfair treatment of employees may adversely affect a firm's ability to get client referrals from other lawyers, which is often a key source of business for firms.

Cost Savings

While firms know they are losing money as they lose associates, few realize the actual amounts lost and the effect on their bottom line. Industry estimates are that it costs between $200,000 and $500,000 to replace a second- or third-year associate. If that sounds high, consider the following costs to a firm from the loss of one associate:
- The lost productivity, calculated at a minimum of 40% of the person's compensation and benefits for each week the position is vacant.
- The costs of recruiting and the training the firm provided.
- The costs of lost knowledge, skills, and contacts that the departing lawyer takes with him or her.
- The costs of losing clients the lawyer will take with him or her.

---

[13] See, e.g., Karen A. Lister, "Firms Develop Initiatives to Keep Women in the Pipelines," *The Houston Lawyer*, May/June 2003, available at http://www.thehoustonlawyer.com/aa_may03/aa_feature/page18/page18.htm; "Greater Diversity Requires Ongoing Commitment and Multiple Approaches," *Metropolitan Corporate Counsel*, March 2003, at 32, available at http://www.beveridgediamond.com/media/news/news.244.pdf.

- The costs of stopping payroll as well as other administrative costs.
- The effect of high attrition on the morale and productivity of the attorneys who remain at the law firm.

To these costs, one must add new hire costs, consisting of:

- Recruiting expenses, including advertisements and interview expenses (e.g., travel, luncheons).
- Search consultant fees and/or referral bonuses.
- Hiring or signing bonuses, bar and moving expenses.
- Interviewing time spent by lawyers at the firm.
- Training costs.
- Lost productivity costs because of an inexperienced attorney or one unfamiliar with the firm's clients, including time written off for getting the new attorney up to speed on client matters.

While each firm will spend different amounts on each of these items, it is easy to see how quickly the costs add up. When multiplied by the number of associates who leave each year, the number gets big enough to capture the attention of even the busiest partner. Firms pay these high amounts over and over again, replacing departing associates with new associates who will also leave within a year or two. To make matters worse, given the current salary levels, these expenses often are incurred before the departing associates even become profitable to the firm.

It is easy to see that implementing a balanced hours program — even if it cuts attrition by only a small amount — would save a firm millions of dollars.

> "A law firm's culture affects its client relationships. If a firm treats its people poorly internally, how could it suppress that externally? It's like any business. If your internal system of how you treat your employees is fundamentally flawed, then the employees' external relationships will reflect that."
>
> — *William J. Flannery, WJF Institute, Austin, Texas*

Improved Morale and Productivity

Turnover breeds discontent. Attorneys who do not leave wonder if they are on a sinking ship and feel burdened as they pick up the work of those who did leave. High turnover also undermines collegiality and mentoring because attorneys are more reluctant to form bonds with colleagues if they suspect those bonds will be short-lived. A balanced hours program that cuts attrition ameliorates these ills. Fundamentally, it adds to the attorneys' sense of well-being because, in addition to fostering relationships with colleagues, it demonstrates to the attorneys that their firm has a supportive culture that responds to their needs. The attorneys feel less stress, which in turn increases their productivity.[14] Productivity is further enhanced by the reduction in attrition-related distractions — rumor mills, farewell parties, assimilation of new attorneys, and the like.

Enhanced Reputation

Firms that adopt balanced hours programs will be viewed favorably in the community. They will be seen as socially responsible, taking care of attorneys' needs, deliberately attracting and retaining diverse attorneys, and eradicating outdated and unfair practices. In addition, providing balanced hour schedules responds to the widespread and uncontroversial sense that children need and deserve time with their parents, and that one's parents and partners deserve time and attention when they are ill. Balanced hours programs permit

---

One Firm's Experience

Pillsbury Winthrop's managing partner, Marina Park, became partner while working part-time. Mary Cranston, Pillsbury's chair, said, "We make sure all the young women know that [nonsupport for attorneys on balanced schedules] is not acceptable — that if there is a problem they should let me or [the head of HR] know. We just have no patience for that here."

"You've got to look at the big picture here. If women or men with family obligations can't find what they need here, they will vote with their feet. You've got to load all of the costs of attrition into the equation. In light of the demographics of who is graduating from law school, firms that get diversity right will have much lower attrition. This more than swamps out the slightly higher overhead costs."

Pillsbury Winthrop, LLP, found that support for balanced schedules "is absolutely positive for the bottom line. During the recent period when the market was aggressive and it was very hard to hang onto lawyers, we lost many fewer associates. We really didn't lose that many women. It gave us a tremendous edge," concluded Cranston.

---

[14] Numerous studies find stress and productivity to be inversely linked. See National Institute for Occupational Health and Safety Job Stress Research Program, available at http://www.cdc.gov/niosh/stresshp.html, for citations.

attorneys to participate in the world outside the law, doing things that are meaningful to them and their communities. Allowing attorneys to meet these moral obligations without having to sacrifice their careers not only recognizes the differing needs of a diverse attorney population, it also promotes the development of well-rounded attorneys. It establishes a firm's reputation for fairness as well.

Sample Award Winners

Law firms that have appeared on *Working Mother Magazine's* 100 Best Companies for Working Mothers list include:

- Arnold & Porter LLP
- Morrison & Foerster LLP

Law firms that have appeared on *Fortune* Magazine's 100 Best Companies to Work for list include:

- Alston & Bird LLP
- Arnold & Porter LLP
- Fenwick & West LLP
- McCutchen, Doyle, Brown & Enersen
- Morrison & Foerster LLP

Law firms that have won the Philadelphia Bar Association's Family Friendly Award include:

- Berner & Klaw
- Eckert Seamans Cherin & Mellott, LLC

Law firms that have won the Bar Association of the District of Columbia's Quality of Life Award include:

- Arnold & Porter LLP
- Dickstein Shapiro Morin & Oshinksy, LLP
- Feldesman, Tucker, Leifer, Fidell & Bank, LLP

Case Studies

Can Firms Really Save Money with Balanced Hours Programs?

Corporate America has realized the benefits of effective work/life programs, as the examples below show. There is every reason to believe that law firms would realize similar benefits.

- Deloitte Touche Tohmatsu has documented that its improved workplace flexibility programs saved it $27 million in 2003 alone. *Better on Balance? The Corporate Counsel Work/Life Report, available at www.pardc.org.*

- Ernst & Young estimates, based on widely accepted estimates of replacement costs of 1.5 times base salary, that the company's workplace flexibility programs and other initiatives aimed at women's development and advancement have saved it an average of $12 million annually in the past seven years. *Better on Balance? The Corporate Counsel Work/Life Report, available at www.pardc.org.*

- The Society for Human Resource Management (SHRM) profiles several companies that have found that improved work/life policies brought them improved employee and customer retention, including Aetna Life & Casualty Co, which "halved the rate of resignations among new mothers by extending its unpaid parental leave to six months, saving it $1 million a year in hiring and training expenses." *Society for Human Resource Management, Integrating Work/Life Programs: SHRM Work/Life Balance Toolkit (2003), available at http://www.shrm.org.*

- First Tennessee Bank calculated that its adoption of flexible schedules and work/life balance policies boosted profits by $106 million over a two-year period. A study by the bank showed a direct correlation between the new work policies and customer retention. *Family Friendly Business Works, Washington Citizen (1999), available at http://www.familiesnorthwest.org/pdf/citizen/nov99.pdf; Michelle Martinez, Work-Life Programs Reap Business Benefits, HR Magazine (Society for Human Resource Management, June 1997).*

Chapter Summary

- → Talented attorneys who are key to law firms' futures are leaving firms because they have not been able to find the work/life balance they need. The departing attorneys are male and female, and are seeking room in their lives for many purposes, not just childcare.

- → Clients are demanding that law firms reduce their attrition. Turnover aggravates clients and weakens their ties to firms.

- → Balanced hours programs are programs that allow attorneys to work reduced hours without stigma and without sacrificing professional success.

- → Firms that implement balanced hours programs will reap a variety of benefits, including improved client relationships and business development, easier recruiting, significant cost savings, and better morale.

Chapter 2

How Current Part-Time Programs Hurt Law Firms

Almost every medium or large-sized law firm has a part-time program,[1] so why aren't the firms realizing the benefits described in the first chapter? Why does attrition remain high? Why do clients increasingly express concern over the high rate of attorney turnover?

Existing part-time programs at law firms not only fail to generate benefits for the firms and their attorneys but in fact *create* problems for the firms and attorneys that exacerbate turnover-related ills. Unfortunately for firm management, these problems are often hidden. Law firm managers may be the last to know that their firms' existing part-time programs are not working because discussion of the problems is perceived as ill-advised.

This chapter will illuminate the problems with existing part-time programs and provide a simple test, the PAR Usability Test, that law firm managers can use to determine if their law firms' policies are up to par.

■ The Problems

Dissatisfaction with a firm's part-time program can affect all of a firm's attorneys, not just those working reduced hours. Problems often arise when a part-time program is put into place without adequate planning, support, training, and supervision. Those working part-time feel betrayed by policies that sound good on paper but in practice fall far short of their promise. Flawed programs also affect attorneys who would like to work part-time but feel they cannot because they fear a part-time schedule might damage their careers. Finally, flawed programs may well affect attorneys who feel they are being made to work longer hours to "pick up the slack" for the part-timers.

---

[1] In 2003, 96.0% of the offices in the *NALP Directory of Legal Employers* reported offering part-time schedules, as compared to 94.5% in 2000. "Availability and Use of Part-Time Provisions in Law Firms — 2003" (NALP, 2003).

Recent studies by PAR and others[2] have documented the widespread problems in part-time programs at a wide range of variously sized law firms across the country. The two primary problems are "schedule creep" and "stigma."

Schedule Creep

Attorneys negotiate reduced hours, only to find that over time their hours creep back up to full-time levels while their pay remains at part-time levels. Schedule creep often stems from unspoken expectations on the part of the firm about what it means to be "committed." Where commitment is confused with schedule, part-time attorneys may well receive informal messages that a part-time attorney will continue to do the same amount of work as when he or she was full-time. To meet these expectations, part-time attorneys may feel the need to work virtually full-time hours in order to prove that they are still valuable team members who can pull their own weight. The result is schedule creep that fans the flames of dissatisfaction and hastens attorney departures from a firm.

Some firms compensate part-time attorneys for the additional hours they work through a "lookback provision." While this is better than not paying for the additional hours, it does not address the fundamental issue: If part-time attorneys wanted more money, they would not have requested a part-time schedule in the first place.

Law firms that do not compensate part-time attorneys for additional work have even more severe problems. In addition to violating their agreements with the part-time attorneys, they may be at risk for an Equal Pay Act lawsuit. At many firms, the part-time attorneys are all female. If they are being paid less than male attorneys for doing the same work — that is, being paid for part-time hours while working full-time hours — the potential for a lawsuit exists.

Schedule creep leads to high attrition, which undermines the retention goals of part-time programs. Some part-time attorneys will feel no choice but to try to live up to workload expectations that are much higher than can reasonably be accomplished part-time, running themselves ragged both physically and mentally until burnout forces them to

---

[2] Deborah L. Rhode, for the ABA Commission on Women and the Profession, *Lawyers and Balanced Lives* (2001); Catalyst, *Women in Law: Making the Case* (2001); Keith Cunningham, "Father Time: Flexible Work Arrangements and the Law Firm's Failure of the Family," *Stanford Law Review* vol. 53:967-1008 (April 2001); Women's Bar Association of Massachusetts, *More Than Part Time: The Effect of Reduced-Hours Arrangements on the Retention, Recruitment, and Success of Women Attorneys in Law Firms* (2000) (available at http://womenlaw.stanford.edu/mass.rpt.html.); Boston Bar Association Task Force on Work-Life Balance, *Facing The Grail: Confronting the Cost of Work-Family Imbalance* (June 1999).

leave. Other part-time attorneys will try to preserve their part-time schedules by seeking to cut back their workload or reschedule events, only to be forced out of the firm as a poor performer who "isn't committed" to the practice of law.

Schedule creep also forces full-time attorneys out the door, because they see their firms' dysfunctional part-time program as unable to solve their needs to balance their lives.

Schedule Creep Scenarios

Obvious examples of schedule creep abound. Many attorneys report working 50 to 60 hours per week on a part-time schedule and getting paid only a percentage of a full-time salary. One attorney worked in excess of 70 hours per week for several weeks while getting paid 80% of a full-time salary.

Refusal to respect part-time schedules is a less obvious schedule creep problem. Supervising attorneys who schedule non-emergency meetings or conference calls for times when part-time attorneys are out of the office send a strong message that firm expectations are inconsistent with the firm's decision to approve a part-time schedule.

Another common scenario occurs when a firm (or an individual supervisor) tells part-time attorneys not to tell clients about their hours of availability. Keeping clients in the dark about a part-time schedule inevitably leads clients to schedule meetings or request work product during times when the attorney is scheduled to be out of the office. One corporate counsel expressed dismay to PAR upon learning, after a long period, that an attorney was working part-time, saying that he would much prefer to have known so that he could respect her schedule where humanly possible.

Stigma

Part-time work is so stigmatized at many law firms that attorneys who wish to reduce their hours leave their firms rather than jeopardize their legal careers. Stigma is evidenced in numerous ways, often within a single firm:

- *Elimination of advancement.* Attorneys perceive that working part-time is the professional "kiss of death" as their opportunities for advancement dry up. At some firms, stigma is official because all part-time attorneys are removed from the partnership track. Most are destined to remain associates, although a few might break through to "of counsel" status. At other firms, part-time attorneys are not formally removed from the partnership track but nevertheless find themselves unable to advance because of a de facto policy of not promoting part-time attorneys to partner. Even at firms that do promote the occasional part-time associate, attorneys report that working part-time typically diminishes their chances of making partner.

- *Loss of status.* By and large, attorneys reach law firms through records of stellar performance. They have been at the top of their classes, developed impressive credentials, and enjoyed many accolades. As a measure of their worth and hard work, they have landed a job at a prestigious firm where they continue to succeed. Yet once they request a part-time schedule, the status ladder becomes a greased pole. No longer working Herculean hours, they find themselves booted from the "star" track. Colleagues view them differently, partners do not seek them out for social or professional events, and no one is hitching a ride on their coattails. Largely, the loss of status is due to the perception that the now part-time attorney does not have much of a future at the firm.

- *Weakened relationships.* Part-time attorneys report that their schedules often have a negative impact on their professional and personal relationships. As they work frantically to accomplish as much work on a part-time schedule as they did on a full-time schedule, time for socializing dries up. Mentoring relationships disappear as part-time attorneys are not perceived as "serious" enough to justify the effort of mentoring. Relationships with colleagues cool as part-timers are seen as not being team players.

- *Transfer from practice area.* Some part-time attorneys have found that their firms require them to switch from practice areas deemed incompatible with part-time work to more "suitable" practice areas, such as switching from litigation to regulatory work. Others have reported being moved to practice areas that were the least popular in the firm or outside the mainstream of the firm's work.

- *Financial penalties.* Historically, most law firms paid part-time attorneys a lower percentage of full-time pay than the percentage of full-time hours they were required to work. Commonly called "the haircut," an attorney would typically be paid 70% of the full-time rate for working 80% of a full-time schedule. The difference was justified by the claim that part-time attorneys cost firms more in terms of overhead. This hours/pay differential has disappeared from many large firms today, perhaps due to recognition that the differential could present problems in an Equal Pay Act suit. Nevertheless, part-time attorneys in today's law firms often still take a financial hit. Many give up some or all of their benefits when they go part-time, and many lose their eligibility for bonuses. In addition, as described in the preceding section about schedule creep, many find themselves working far more hours than those for which they are paid. Getting paid less for working close to full time — and being taken off the partnership track to boot — is an all too common recipe for attrition.

- *Diminished quality of assignments.* A large proportion of part-time attorneys say that the quality of their assignments decreased dramatically when they changed their schedule. They found they were no longer serving the firm's high-profile clients and were not put on cases that involved travel; instead, requests for research memos and document reviews filled their "in" baskets. Similarly, assignments to firm committees frequently dried up. In part, the diminished quality of assignments may be due to supervising attorneys' well-meaning but misguided attempts to accommodate reduced schedules. The quality of assignments an attorney receives is directly related to the attorney's professional development and readiness for advancement, so diminished assignments exacerbate the advancement difficulties part-timers face.

- *Lost professional development.* The professional development of part-time attorneys will suffer, of course, if they are not given challenging work. Yet the loss of professional development goes deeper at many firms. Part-time attorneys have found themselves ineligible for continuing legal education unless they pay for it themselves and attend sessions on their own time. Similarly, some are not permitted to work for bar associations or community organizations and (unlike their full-time counterparts) are not permitted to do pro bono work during office time.

Real-Life Stigma

Some quotes from part-time attorneys:

- "I used to feel I was a valued and well regarded member of the firm. Now I feel as if I am an outcast."

- "I worked full-time at first, and then switched to part-time after my first child was born. Everything changed once I moved to part-time. I was taken off all firm committees, and one partner didn't want to work with me any more — he said it was because I couldn't travel, although he never asked me if I could still travel. I was given work in an area in which I had no background. It was a type of work that the other associates hated. After a while, the partner in charge became more supportive of me, once he saw that I would still work hard to meet deadlines. Eventually, though, it became harder to stay at a firm that viewed me as a second-class citizen, and I left."

- "The head of the litigation department decided that the best way to use someone in my anomalous (part-time) position was to assign me sole responsibility for the smaller, less sophisticated matters (or, to put it more bluntly, the 'dog cases') that the litigation department took on more or less as a favor for clients of the firm's business department. Once I figured this out, it wasn't long before I started looking for another job."

- "One part-time lawyer found to her surprise that they had forgotten to invite her to the practice group retreat. They had invited male attorneys far junior to her, but they forgot to invite her." *(Law Firm Consultant)*

- "[Going part-time] has destroyed [my career] for all intents and purposes. It has completely, utterly, and irreversibly altered my future, my practice, my finances, my reputation, my relationships, and my friendships." *(A partner who had worked with a firm for 20 years, quoted in* More Than Part-Time.*)*

- "Since I came back from maternity leave, I get the work of a paralegal. I want to say: 'Look, I had a baby, not a lobotomy.'"

The Communication Gap

Law firm managers are quick to say that schedule creep and stigma do not exist at their firms — and they sincerely believe this. On several occasions during PAR's study, interviews with a law firm managing partner and separate interviews with attorneys at the same firm produced dramatically different views about the causes of attrition, the state of attorney morale, and the effectiveness of part-time programs. There is little mystery about the cause of the disconnect. Attorneys believe that pointing out the firm's shortcomings would brand them as "whiny," or as "not a team player." Discussing the shortcomings of part-time programs carries the additional risk of being viewed as someone who doesn't want to pull his or her own weight, someone who puts other interests ahead of working for the firm. It is imperative that those who lead law firms find a way to hear what the attorneys won't tell them.

The PAR Usability Test

The PAR Usability Test will let law firm managers know if a communication gap exists with respect to the effectiveness of their firms' part-time programs. Using easily obtained and objective data, the Usability Test will show whether a firm's program is up to par, or whether it is marred by stigma and schedule creep. Where schedule creep and stigma exist, a part-time program may not just be failing to keep good attorneys; it may be driving them away.

The PAR Usability Test

1. Usage rate, broken down by sex.
2. Median number of hours worked and duration of the balanced hours schedule.
3. Schedule creep.
4. Comparison of the assignments of balanced hours attorneys before, and after, they reduced their hours.
5. Comparative promotion rates of attorneys on standard and balanced hours schedules.
6. Comparative attrition rates of attorneys on standard and balanced hours schedules.

Copyright 2001 Joan Williams. Reprinted with permission.

1. Usage Rate Broken Down by Sex

A part-time program does little good if no one uses it, and lack of use is a key indicator of the health of the program.

To find your firm's usage rate, take the total number of attorneys working part-time and divide it by the total number of attorneys at your firm (partners, associates, counsel). What are usage rates for good part-time programs? For professional workers as a whole, 2000 survey data from the Bureau of Labor Statistics show that approximately 13% work part-time. For the legal profession, a 2003 analysis by NALP showed an astonishingly low percentage of associates and partners working part-time: only 4.1% of all attorneys at law firms in the *NALP Directory of Legal Employers*.[3] By contrast, firms with effective part-time programs have much higher usage rates: Arnold & Porter in Washington, D.C. has a usage rate of almost 8%; Mintz, Levin, Cohn, Ferris, Glovsky & Popeo in Boston has a rate of more than 9%; and Palmer and Dodge in Boston has a rate of 12%.[4]

Once you have figured out your part-time usage rate, break it down by sex. Men are much less likely than women to work in positions that are stigmatized and that offer little advancement potential. If virtually no men work part-time at your firm, you should be concerned about whether your part-time program marginalizes those who use it.

Some firms believe that if they have one or two women who are successfully working part-time, they have a good part-time program. Rarely is that true. One or two success stories are much more likely to be a sign of the "superstar" problem: treating star performers exceptionally well while disregarding the needs of other workers. The superstar problem lulls firms into complacency, damages morale with the appearance of favoritism, and ultimately drives from the firm the vast majority of the attorneys who need to have balance in their lives.

A comparison of two fairly typical law firm part-time programs is shown in the box on the opposite page. The usage rates indicate that firm B has a more usable part-time program.

---

[3] "Availability and Use of Part-Time Provisions in Law Firms — 2003" (NALP, 2003).
[4] *More Than Part Time*, supra, n.2, at 13; *NALP Directory of Legal Employers* (2001).

Comparison of Two Firms' Part-Time Programs

Firm A		Firm B	
Number of associates:	72	Number of associates:	72
Number of counsel:	9	Number of counsel:	9
Number of partners:	39	Number of partners:	39
Total attorneys:	120	Total attorneys:	120
Number of associates working part-time:	2	Number of associates working part-time:	8
Number of counsel working part-time:	2	Number of counsel working part-time:	4
Number of partners working part-time:	0	Number of partners working part-time:	3
Usage rate:	3.3%	Usage rate:	12.5%
Number of men working part-time:	0	Number of men working part-time:	4

2. Median Number of Hours Worked and Duration of the Balanced Hours Schedule

Another key indicator of the health of a firm's part-time program is how many hours part-time attorneys work on average and for how many months or years attorneys remain on a part-time schedule. Median part time schedules at law firms are often in excess of what would be considered full-time in the world outside of law firms: 80% of a typical full-time 60-hour week is 48 hours per week, a schedule many attorneys do not consider a suitable balance between work and family (or other) obligations. In addition, law firms frequently limit the length of time that an attorney can work part-time, either explicitly through the firm's policy or implicitly through withholding benefits, opportunities for professional development, and advancement until an attorney returns to full-time. The reasons attorneys seek to reduce their hours, such as for child rearing, elder care, or health concerns, typically cannot be assigned a defined ending date, and the short duration of part-time schedules will undermine the effectiveness of a part-time program. A study of part-time lawyers in Boston found that the *average* time period a partner worked part-time was seven years.[5]

---

[5] *More Than Part Time, supra,* n.2, at 14.

To find your firm's median number of hours worked, list the yearly total hours worked by each part-time attorney from least to greatest and find the mid-point. Similarly, to find the median duration of part-time schedules, list the length of time worked on a part-time schedule by each attorney who is now working part-time or who has worked part-time in the recent past (perhaps in the last five years or so); list these times from least to greatest and find the mid-point. (The median is chosen instead of the mean because this makes it less likely that the short hours or long duration of one person's schedule will give a false impression of the experience of balanced hours attorneys considered as a group.) A median of 60-80% of full-time schedules signals an effective part-time program, as does a median duration of several years.

Calculation of median schedules and durations is demonstrated in the example below.

Sample Calculation of Median Schedules and Durations

Median Part-Time Schedule	Median Duration of Part-Time Schedule
Part-Time Attorney 1 works 27 hrs/week	Part-Time Attorney 1 worked part-time for 6 months
Part-Time Attorney 2 works 30 hrs/week	Part-Time Attorney 2 worked part-time for 13 months
Part-Time Attorney 3 works 36 hrs/week	Part-Time Attorney 3 worked part-time for 22 months
Part-Time Attorney 4 works 38 hrs/week	Part-Time Attorney 4 worked part-time for 48 months
Part-Time Attorney 5 works 48 hrs/week	Part-Time Attorney 5 worked part-time for 61 months
Median is 36 hrs/week — or 60% of a 60-hour week	Median is 22 months

3. Schedule Creep

Deliberately or not, regularly requiring part-time attorneys to work more hours than the schedule they have been promised guarantees the failure of any part-time program. Schedule creep is one of the complaints most frequently raised by part-time attorneys, as well as by attorneys who would like to work part-time but believe it is better to quit than to work full-time for part-time pay.

Measuring schedule creep is easy. Look at the number of hours each part-time attorney has agreed to work, and compare it to the number of hours he or she regularly works. If the comparison shows that attorneys on nonstandard schedules are consistently working more hours than the schedule they have been promised, then schedule creep is undermining the effectiveness and usability of the policy.

There will be times, of course, when a true crisis arises; part-time attorneys are professionals who will maintain the flexibility needed to handle whatever crises may occur. The key is reciprocity. Once the crisis is over, is that attorney free to take "comp time" without having this interpreted as a lack of commitment? Does the supervisor of a balanced hours attorney consider it part of his or her management responsibility to ensure that crises really are unavoidable, rather than a mere failure to anticipate predictable workflow issues?

Looking at hours budgeted and worked over a period of months will show whether excess hours reflect a crisis or ongoing schedule creep. It will also show whether the part-time attorney has been permitted to take comp time to offset extra hours worked in a crisis. An example is provided below.

Examples of Measuring Schedule Creep

Schedule Creep Exists	No Schedule Creep Exists
Part-Time Attorney 1 is budgeted to work 32 hours per week. He works as follows:	Part-Time Attorney 2 is budgeted to work 32 hours per week. He works as follows:
Week 1 — 33 hours	Week 1 — 32 hours
Week 2 — 37 hours	Week 2 — 33 hours
Week 3 — 42 hours	Week 3 — 46 hours
Week 4 — 34 hours	Week 4 — 24 hours
Week 5 — 46 hours	Week 5 — 30 hours
Week 6 — 47 hours	Week 6 — 30 hours
Week 7 — 37 hours	Week 7 — 30 hours
Week 8 — 40 hours	Week 8 — 32 hours
High level of schedule creep	**Low level of schedule creep**

4. Comparison of the Assignments of Balanced Hours Attorneys Before, and After, They Reduced Their Hours

If part-time attorneys do not get quality work assignments — and many report they do not — their professional development will stagnate. Moreover, if they are shifted to nothing more than low-level, routine matters, they will become disenchanted and leave the firm.

Comparing the type of work, level of responsibility, and amount of client contact part-time attorneys had before, and after, changing their schedules is also relatively easy. To compare work assignments, look at the billing records of part-time attorneys. If too much rote work (e.g., document reviews, form preparation) and too little client contact is evident, your firm's policies are likely not effective and usable. For new hires, assignments can be compared to those of other attorneys at the same level in the same practice group. Another good way to judge whether part-time attorneys are being pushed to the sidelines is to follow the lead of Deloitte Touche Tohmatsu and look at your firm's largest and highest-profile matters to make sure that part-time attorneys are on the teams handling those matters. It is still necessary to look at the type of work performed, however, to ensure that the part-time attorneys are not handling a disproportionate amount of rote work.

5. Comparative Promotion Rates of Attorneys on Standard and Balanced Hours Schedules

As noted, numerous attorneys view reduced hours work as ending all hope of partnership. The fact that only 15 to 16% of law firm partners are women,[6] despite decades of law schools graduating nearly equal percentages of women and men, shows they may be right.

Firms that have a policy of not promoting part-time attorneys to partner already know what a comparison of promotion rates would show. Firms that do not formally remove part-time attorneys from the partnership track are not always aware of large disparities in the promotion rates of part-time and full-time attorneys, and may believe that part-time status is not career-ending when in practice it is. Uncovering such disparities is critical; lawyers will be discouraged from using a part-time program if part-timers virtually never *in fact* make partner even if in theory they are eligible to do so.

If your firm allows part-time attorneys to be partners, test whether you have a de facto removal policy by comparing the promotion rates of attorneys on part-time schedules to

---

[6] In 1998, 14.55% of partners in law firms listed in the *NALP Directory of Legal Employers* were women. The number has risen slightly since then: 1999 — 15.04%; 2000 — 15.63%; 2001 — 15.8%; 2002 — 16.3%; 2003 — 16.81%. NALP Research, available at http://www.nalp.org/nalpresearch/mw_indx.htm.

those on full-time schedules. While the promotion rate will not necessarily be identical for these two groups, a persistent imbalance in favor of full-time attorneys may well indicate that part-time attorneys are being penalized in terms of promotions.

6. Comparative Attrition Rates of Attorneys on Standard and Balanced Hours Schedules

Ample evidence exists that a usable and effective part-time program can effect sharp cuts in attrition. However, a program plagued by stigma and schedule creep may actually exacerbate attrition. In a 2001 study, the Massachusetts Women's Bar Association[7] found that, given the problems with existing part-time policies, attrition rates among part-time attorneys were even higher than among other attorneys. The Association found, for example, that in 1997 and 1998, men with standard schedules had an attrition rate of 9% and women with standard schedules had an attrition rate of 12%, but women working reduced hours had an attrition rate of almost 23%.[8] Comparing attrition rates allows a firm to assess the need for further investigation to identify problems with its part-time program.

To make the comparison, gather attrition data for men working full-time, women working full-time, men working part-time, and women working part-time. Given the intense demand for reduced hours, if the attrition rate among attorneys working reduced hours is significantly higher than that of the full-time groups, this signals problems with your firm's part-time policy.

■ So How Are Balanced Hours Programs Different?

Firms that provide balanced hours can expect to retain talented attorneys whom they would otherwise lose due to lifestyle issues. Balanced hours programs differ from traditional part-time programs in a number of ways. First, balanced hours programs are driven by firms' business needs and are not merely accommodations that must be tolerated. Reduced schedules are adopted as an acceptable workstyle in order to assure the long-term health of the firm, but individual attorneys reduce their hours only after they and their supervisors create a business plan that demonstrates how the work will get done and how client needs will be met.

Second, the hallmark of balanced hours programs is separation of the concepts of an attorney's value to the firm and the schedule the attorney can work. In recognizing that quality matters more than face time, a firm recognizes that attorneys who do good work

---

[7] *More Than Part Time*, supra, n.2.
[8] Id. at App. B, chart 3.

and have good relationships with clients are valuable assets of the firm and should be retained even if they do not work what is considered a full-time schedule.

Third, balanced hours programs are not stigmatized. The firm and attorneys work to ensure that balanced hours attorneys are not punished or marginalized because of the schedules they keep. Firm leaders send the message that balanced hours are accepted by the firm. Assignments, client contact, status within the firm, and relationships with colleagues and superiors are unaffected by the number of hours an attorney works.

Fourth, balanced hours programs treat attorneys proportionally. Attorneys who reduce their hours have their salaries reduced only proportionally, and they continue to progress professionally toward partnership or within partnership tiers. Their workload is reduced proportionally with their hours to ensure successful implementation of the attorneys' reduced schedules, but their assignments remain challenging and interesting.

Finally, balanced hours programs treat attorneys fairly. Reduced schedules are available to all attorneys, and allow attorneys to establish flexible schedules that meet their personal needs while ensuring that client needs are met. Gone are traditional notions that only mothers can work part-time and only while their children are young, and that part-time means working a rigid schedule that would still be considered full-time in other areas of the economy. Fairness is also evident in the active prevention of schedule creep, which ensures that firms that have made an agreement with attorneys regarding reduced hours keep their end of the bargain.

 **Chapter Summary**

→ Law firm managers are often unaware of the dissatisfaction caused by their existing part-time programs.

→ The main causes of dissatisfaction are schedule creep and stigma. Schedule creep is the tendency of part-time hours to creep up to full-time hours, typically with part-time pay. Stigma includes formal or de facto removal from the partnership track, lack of respect from colleagues, destruction of mentoring and social relationships, poor quality work assignments, diminished opportunities for CLE, pro bono work, and bar work, and financial penalties.

→ Law firm managers can overcome the communication gap and uncover the existence of problems with their firms' part-time programs. The first step is to take the PAR Usability Test, which uses objective and easily obtained data to measure the following:

1. Usage rate, broken down by sex.
2. Median number of hours worked and duration of the balanced hours schedule.
3. Schedule creep.
4. Comparison of the assignments of balanced hours attorneys before, and after, they reduced their hours.
5. Comparative promotion rates of attorneys on standard and balanced hours schedules.
6. Comparative attrition rates of attorneys on standard and balanced hours schedules.

→ Balanced hours programs differ from traditional part-time programs in that they respond to business needs, separate the worth of an attorney from the number of hours the attorney works, do not stigmatize those who reduce their hours, and treat all attorneys proportionally and fairly.

Chapter 3

The Myth of Unprofitability

Firms say it many different ways:

- "Part-time costs too much."
- "Part-time attorneys don't make enough money to cover their overhead."
- "I can make more money from an attorney working 100% than one working 80%."

We call statements like this the "Myth of Unprofitability." Like any myth, it has arisen as a simplified explanation not grounded in fact and has attained sacred status through repetition.

The Myth of Unprofitability is based on three fallacies: high lawyer productivity, which means high billable hours, is the only way for a firm to be profitable; lawyers are fungible automatons for whom an hour in the office is an hour billed; and part-time lawyers generate less revenue than their overhead. This chapter will look at the realities that dispel these fallacies.

■ Fallacy #1: High Lawyer Productivity Is the Only Path to Firm Profitability

Law firm profitability is driven by productivity, margin, and leverage, says law firm consultant and former Harvard Business School professor David Maister.[1] As he uses the terms, "productivity" means revenue — or billable hours times hourly rate. "Margin" refers to the level of revenue after expenses are deducted. "Leverage" is the effective use of associate time.

Maister points out that different practice units and different partners can achieve profitability in various ways. A partner may have a high productivity/low leverage practice in which she services her clients herself and bills many hours at a high hourly billing rate. This is the type of partner who is traditionally viewed by firms as being profitable, and firms seek to have as many partners in this mode as possible. Yet, as Maister points out, a partner may make just as much profit for a firm if he has a low productivity/high leverage practice in which he bills fewer hours and uses associate time extensively and effectively,

---

[1] David Maister, *Managing the Professional Service Firm* (Simon & Schuster, 1997), chapter 3.

as many senior partners do. A high-margin practice, where costs are relatively low, can also be profitable even with modest productivity and leverage.[2]

Despite the importance of margin and leverage to a firm's profitability, law firm accounting reports typically highlight only productivity.[3] The contributions of the high productivity partners are recognized in billable hours reports that are circulated monthly, and partner compensation is based largely on the amount of revenue generated by those billable hours. The costs incurred to generate the revenue and the successful generation of revenue from associates typically goes unnoticed.

Emphasizing only one of the profitability factors is a mistake that will cost a firm long-term profitability, according to Maister. Maister uses the example of focusing on margin; costs can be cut only so much and after the bare-bones state is reached, the firm cannot achieve profitability that increases yearly simply by cutting expenses.[4] Similarly, focusing on productivity, as law firms do, is a dead-end. If every attorney in a firm is required to bill more hours per year, the profits per partner will go up for a while. Such a strategy cannot sustain a pattern of increasing profits for the firm over the long-term, however. There are only so many hours in a year, and burnout, attrition, and the availability of work will all prevent long-term increasing profitability. Over the last several years, firms that have tried this approach have seen its shortcomings first-hand.

Encouraging and rewarding high-margin and high-leverage practices as well as productive practices is the strategy for long-term profitability. The benefits to a firm of having balanced hours work would be recognized under such a strategy. Balanced hours attorneys will stay with a firm for a longer period of time, enabling them to achieve the experience and seniority necessary to leverage their practices. They will create and maintain client relationships over the long haul, thereby increasing the firm's client base. By trimming the very high costs of attrition, they help to increase margins. Productivity is also present for balanced hours attorneys, as is discussed below, because more of their in-office time is likely to be spent on billable work and they can command higher hourly fees as they develop their practices.

■ Fallacy #2: Lawyers Are Fungible Billing Machines for Whom an Hour in the Office Is an Hour Billed

While law firm management may talk about lawyers as if they are fungible, if the idea is examined, they must admit that it is not so. If lawyers were truly fungible, firms would not need to spend so many resources hiring lawyers with sterling credentials, desirable

---

[2] Id at 31.
[3] Id at 32.
[4] Id.

skills and experience, and actual or potential business development abilities. Clients would not care who provided services to them, and firms would feel little pain when good attorneys left.

Similarly, lawyers are not mere billing machines (despite lawyer jokes to the contrary); lawyers who work long hours must socialize, take care of personal matters, and relax while in the office.[5] As noted elsewhere, lawyers also have many nonbillable, work-related duties that take up their time. While the mental image of the faceless lawyer drone chained to a desk, pencil gripped in teeth and head bowed over book or keyboard, may be real for some lawyers some of the time, it is certainly not true for all lawyers all of the time.

Statements such as "I'd rather have a 100% lawyer than an 80% lawyer" make sense, however, only if lawyers are interchangeable without regard to their individual strengths and relationships. Such statements not only confuse face time with productivity, but they

---

Full-time Hours Don't Mean Full-time Billing

Experience shows that full-time attorneys are not billing full-time; they frequently spend a portion of their office time socializing with colleagues, resting, and attending to personal matters. As *Wall Street Journal* columnist Sue Shellenbarger has observed of corporate workers, "It may be the worst-kept secret in the workplace: People are working more undertime — stealing time off during the day to compensate for heavier workloads and more stress. Undertime can take many forms, from hours spent away from the office on errands or shopping to chunks of time spent at your desk surfing the Internet." Examples of undertime include naps, working on a book, test driving cars, and exercising.[6] The actual number of hours billed by full-time and part-time attorneys, therefore, may not be dramatically different. As one part-time attorney observed, "I do just as much personal stuff as full-time lawyers, but I'm just more honest about it [by being part-time]."

---

[5] The reality of "downtime on company time" — the need of employees to take extended breaks for such activities as exercise, running personal errands, and resting during the work day — has been recognized in several recent articles. See, e.g., Sue Shellenbarger, "What You Need to Know about Undertime Rules" (April 2002) and "What You Can Get Away With" (May 2002), available online at www.careerjournal.com; "Work/Life Solutions: A Real Benefit for Employees" (Jan. 2001), available at http://www.onesmallstep.org/labor_law.html (workers bank, pay bills, shop, arrange child and elder care, and make travel and event plans on company time).

[6] Sue Shellenbarger, "What You Need to Know about Undertime Rules," supra.

ignore that an 80% lawyer with six solid years of experience and great client relationships is far more valuable than a new 100% lawyer who cranks out work for a few years and quits.

■ Fallacy #3: Part-time Lawyers Generate Less Revenue than Their Overhead

"Overhead" is a malleable term that means different things at different firms. A typical definition is all of the expenses a firm incurs (other than reimbursed expenses incurred on behalf of a client) divided pro rata among all of the attorneys who work at the firm. Its major components include rent, staff salaries and benefits, insurance, furniture and equipment, and utilities. In most firms, overhead is distributed pro rata, despite the fact that revenues are not. This ignores that different attorneys incur expenses on behalf of the firm at different rates. At many firms, partners have bigger offices and either have their own secretaries or share secretaries with fewer other attorneys, whereas associates have small offices and share their secretaries with three or more attorneys. Also, at many firms, rainmakers have much higher expenses related to business development than do partners and associates who are not bringing in business.

While an attorney who reduces the number of hours he or she spends in the office may well reduce the amount of hours-based revenue he or she generates — unless the hours that are cut are nonbillable or the attorney works on a flat-fee basis — it does not necessarily follow that he or she does not generate revenue in excess of expenses. Some expenses are fixed and do not decrease if an attorney decreases his or her hours; examples of this are rent (assuming that office space is not shared) and malpractice insurance. Other expenses

Why Is Overhead Even an Issue?

With the rise in the 1980s of the billable hour and the notion that law is a business, the concept of "overhead" became popular. It was an accounting concept used by firm administrators to reflect the fact that it costs money to make money and that firms have certain fixed costs that could be attributed to the attorneys making the money. Over the years, the "overhead figure" became a shorthand way of accounting for these costs, a way to reflect the costs pro rata rather than using a more time-consuming approach of figuring out how much of the firm's expenses were attributable to each individual attorney. Although this is nothing more than a convenient way to view costs, it has achieved sacred stature, and firms now regularly make business decisions based on the single issue of whether attorneys generate income in excess of the average per-attorney overhead number.

can decrease as an attorney's hours decrease; these include salary and benefits, utilization of support staff, computerized legal research, use of conference rooms, and office supplies. Therefore, the first step in assessing whether the balanced hours attorney generates revenue in excess of expenses is to look at the actual expenses attributable to that attorney and the actual revenue generated. If industry survey data are reliable guideposts,[7] the calculation will likely show that a reduced hours associate generates about $425,000 in revenue and has expenses (including salary and benefits) of about $225,000.[8] Clearly, revenue exceeds expenses and the attorney is generating a profit for the firm.

Excess Costs?

"How much money are we talking about? In 2001, according to a survey of law firm economics I saw recently, average occupancy cost per lawyer in large law firms was $41,000, and the average malpractice premium per lawyer was $4,000. If we assume a part-time lawyer working 75% of the hours of a full-time lawyer, that means that the part-time lawyer is incurring $10,000 in occupancy cost and $1,000 in malpractice insurance expense more than would be the case if it were possible to reduce those costs pro rata with the lawyer's reduced schedule. But what revenue is that lawyer generating, and how does this $11,000 in 'excess' cost compare to that revenue? The same survey showed that average revenue per lawyer at large firms last year was $533,000. Using that figure, a lawyer working a 75% schedule would, on average, generate $400,000 in revenue. The $11,000 in so-called additional cost looks immaterial to me when other relevant numbers are known."

— Excerpt from presentation of James Sandman, managing partner of Arnold & Porter, LLP, at "Summit on Keeping Her in Her Place: New Challenges to the Integration of Women in the Profession," ABA Annual Meeting, Washington, DC, August 11, 2002.

---

[7] Altman Weil, Inc., PricewaterhouseCoopers, and others conduct annual surveys of law firm revenue and expenses. Summaries of Altman Weil surveys can be viewed at http://www.martindale.com/xp/Martindale/Legal_Careers/Job_Seekers/Compensation/comps/financials.xml, and http://www.altmanweil.com/pdf/2002SLFEExecutiveSummary-Final.pdf.

[8] These numbers assume that the associate is in a large firm working 80% time, is paid $100,000 in salary and an additional $40,000 in benefits, and incurs expenses for $40,000 in rent, $4,000 in malpractice insurance, $30,000 in proportional support staff costs, and $11,000 in utilities, office supplies, subscriptions, and equipment.

Sometimes, however, when one says that a reduced hours attorney is more expensive for a firm, one means that a reduced hours attorney generates less revenue than a full-time attorney. Again, actual numbers need to be examined to determine if such a statement can hold up. As noted in the previous section, being in the office full-time does not always equate to billing full-time hours; downtime and the availability of work may well limit the number of hours billed by a full-time attorney. Thus, even "full-time" associates may not be billing at the "full-time" level. While we are loathe to set up an expectation that part-time attorneys will work harder and bill a higher proportion of the hours they spend in the office, it is often the reality that part-time attorneys are able to take care of their personal errands on their own time and do in fact spend a higher percentage of office time actually billing.

In addition, billing rates have to be taken into account. In firms with non-stigmatized part-time programs, part-time attorneys often stay at the firm longer than full-time attorneys, and therefore have more experience and can command a higher billing rate. For example, a part-time senior associate who bills 30 hours a week at $450 per hour generates more revenue ($675,000 annually) than a new associate who bills 40 hours per week at $250 per hour ($500,000 annually). Thus, while it may often be true that a full-time attorney will generate more revenue than a balanced hours attorney, no blanket assumptions can be made.

■ Overhead vs. Personnel

Apart from the issue of whether the "unmet overhead" claim is accurate, there is the fundamental issue of whether the overhead argument should ever be used to deny a part-time work schedule to an attorney. Firms often make decisions in derogation of the "overhead" argument in contexts apart from part-time work. For example, a firm may decide to have a partner dedicated to providing and supervising pro bono work. Though this partner will rarely directly bring in enough money to cover his or her "overhead," he or she is nonetheless very valuable to the firm. Pro bono partners enhance a firm's ability to attract top law school recruits because they demonstrate the firm's dedication to pro bono and the firm's values, which are often important to recruits. Pro bono partners also enhance a firm's reputation in the community as a responsible business citizen, and can generate awards and other positive publicity for the firm. The value of a pro bono partner, financially and otherwise, cannot be denied.

Other examples come readily to mind. Many firms maintain practice areas that do not generate large amounts of revenue but that improve client relationships by allowing the firms to provide a full range of services or by enhancing the firms' reputations. A wills and trusts attorney, for example, may or may not make enough money to cover overhead at a large law firm, but the attorney can be invaluable in maintaining client relationships by making it unnecessary for the client to go to another firm to create a trust. Similarly, some large firms have celebrity attorneys who may not generate significant revenue on their own but who add to the firms' stature and ability to attract new clients.

Firms that make such "uneconomic" decisions recognize that requiring each individual attorney to be a short-term profit center for the firm is not necessarily the path to financial health. They take a long view, asking what an attorney, over the lifetime of his or her career, will bring to the firm. They may also take a long view of the firm's needs, and ask whether it is possible to attract and retain the highest quality workforce if the firm prioritizes attorneys' abilities to be short-term profit centers over their abilities to provide other value to the firm. Requests for balanced hours schedules should be viewed similarly.

■ The Bottom Line

Alison Hooker of Ernst & Young has said, "Often times it is the internal accounting practices that ensure that part-time employment will be infeasible. If one looks at the underlying cost allocation issues, much of this can be corrected." Although accounting procedures used by many law firms equate revenue and profitability, sound accounting principles demand that costs as well as revenue be taken into account. The standard business model assesses not revenue alone but the bottom line.

Even if firms decide that they cannot recognize the non-revenue benefits of part-time attorneys, and even if firms decide to take a short-term view and use overhead as a personnel decision-making tool, the fact remains that any lack of profitability these firms perceive will be offset by the amount saved through reduced recruiting costs and by the amount generated through more stable client relationships. Moreover, even if a part-time attorney brings in less revenue, the attorney is still with the firm and the firm has not had to incur costs to replace him or her. Improved retention is part of an overall move toward cost reduction that will improve a firm's bottom line.

 **Chapter Summary**

→ Firm profitability is based on productivity, margin, and leverage. Law firm reporting and rewarding is typically limited to productivity, which produces only short-term profits. Balanced hours attorneys appear not to be profitable when productivity is the only factor measured, but looking at margin and leverage and planning for the long term shows their value.

→ Lawyers are not fungible. Individual experiences, relationships, and skills make lawyers unique, and firms cannot simply trade a part-time lawyer for a full-time lawyer.

→ Part-time attorneys are likely to bring in more revenue than their overhead costs, even if the amount of overhead assigned to them is the same as to full-time attorneys. Current conventions for calculating overhead are conventions that may well distort the contribution of part-time attorneys to a firm's long-term financial health. Overhead is a malleable concept that focuses only on margin and the short term.

→ When all is said and done, even if firms insist on measuring only productivity and making personnel decisions based on margin, firms still profit by offering balanced hours because the saved attrition costs far outweigh any reduction in revenue.

Part Two:
Creating and Implementing Balanced Hours Programs

Chapter 4

Laying the Foundation for a Balanced Hours Program

A successful balanced hours program, like a building, requires a solid foundation. The foundation is made not of concrete and steel, but of strategic planning and thoughtful implementation. Yet most law firms that have adopted part-time policies have overlooked this requirement and have ended up with a shelf policy instead of a business-enhancing program — a house of cards rather than a house.

Successful corporations that undertake new initiatives aimed at improving their business spend months planning and implementing the initiatives. Numerous books and articles exist to advise businesses on how to effect change within their organizations,[1] and strategically preparing for change is recognized as so important that business schools now offer graduate courses focused solely on managing change.[2] Experts in change dynamics counsel that spadework up front — articulating the need for a new program, creating a coalition to implement the program, and engaging in strategic planning — is essential to success.[3]

Spadework is no less important to law firms, yet many look only for a quick fix that consists of nothing more than calling PAR or a neighboring law firm and asking for a policy that they can stick in their employee handbooks. The written policy is not what matters, however. *Implementation of the policy is what will produce benefits for the firm.*

---

[1] E.g., John P. Kotter and Dan S. Cohen, *The Heart of Change: Real-Life Stories of How People Change Their Organizations* (Harvard Business School Press, 2002); Leon De Caluwe and Hans Vermaak, *Learning to Change: A Guide for Organizational Change Agents* (Sage Publications, 2002); Donald Hambrick, David A. Nadler, and Michael L. Tushman, editors, *Navigating Change: How CEOs, Top Teams, and Boards Steer Transformation* (Harvard Business School Press, 1998); John P. Kotter, *Leading Change* (Harvard Business School Press, 1996); Lance Berger and Martin Sikora, editors, *The Change Management Handbook* (Irwin Professional Publishing, 1994); Gordon Donaldson, *Corporate Restructuring: Managing the Change Process from Within* (Harvard Business School Press, 1994).

[2] E.g., Harvard Business School, The Wharton School, and The Fuqua School of Business (Duke University) all offer courses in leading organizational change.

[3] E.g., John P. Kotter, *Leading Change* (Harvard Business School Press, 1996).

Implementation requires careful planning to ensure success and to minimize disruptions to the work of the law firm. It requires communication of the reasons for the change, including how the changes will benefit both the firm and individual attorneys. Most fundamentally, it requires commitment, consistency, and persistence. The goal of implementation is to make the new program "stick" — to make it become part of the fabric of the firm so the firm's business goals will be realized.

This chapter sets forth steps in the early spadework that will set the stage for successful implementation.

■ Initial Considerations

Don't Expect Quick Success

Implementing new programs is not easy. New programs mean change, which takes time away from other work and may make some lawyers uneasy. People are naturally resistant to change, and attorneys are no exception. Busy schedules provide a ready-made excuse to avoid change. Eccentric personalities, territorial chieftains, and sticks-in-the-mud may try to unite to rebuff change efforts. Recognizing this from the outset will dispel unrealistic expectations. It will also allow the firm to identify potential obstacles and resistance, and to plan accordingly.

Those who are in charge of initiating the balanced hours program should think realistically about how long it will take for the new program to be introduced to the firm and to take root. A schedule that allows six months of spadework before a balanced hours policy is introduced and another six months for it to be implemented is probably realistic for many medium- to large-sized firms, but the schedule for any particular firm will depend on its individual needs and quirks.

Recognize the Level of Effort That Will Be Required

Successful implementation is going to require time and effort. Some of the work may be streamlined by bringing in outside consultants, but it will nevertheless take time away from other work. At the outset, individuals involved in the effort will want to set aside time in their schedules and perhaps even temporarily reduce other nonbillable work that they do for the firm. It would be prudent to carve out one or two hours per week.

Articulate Why the Firm Needs a Balanced Hours Program

At this preliminary stage, articulating why the firm needs a balanced hours program will help to build the foundation. Later, a full assessment of the firm's starting position and of what the firm can hope to remedy with or to gain from a balanced hours program will be essential. For now, informally gathering data on recent attrition, the success of recruiting efforts, expressions from associates regarding the need for balance, and expressions from clients regarding attrition will be enough to get started.

> **Some Data to Gather**
>
> - Names of clients who have stated diversity objectives for hiring outside counsel.
> - Number of women and minority partners at the firm.
> - Names of clients who have switched to another firm for diversity or attrition reasons.
> - Number of attorneys who have left the firm in the past year.
> - Number of attorneys currently working part-time, broken down by sex and position (associate, partner, counsel).
> - Number of offers made last year to new attorneys and number accepted.
> - List of schools and clerkships from which the new attorneys came.
> - Comments made by attorneys about schedules, part-time, quality of life, and morale.

■ Build the Foundation

In the initial stages, there are likely to be just one or two individuals at a firm who have assessed the firm's needs and decided to move forward with a balanced hours program. Such individuals can get the ball rolling by broadening the involvement of others in the firm.

Identify the Firm's Key Players

No new program is going to work in a law firm or elsewhere unless it has the unqualified support of top management and of the individuals who wield the most power. Some of the most important spadework will identify these individuals and help them to understand the benefits to the firm that a balanced hours program can bring.

> "Failure [to produce change] is usually associated with underestimating the difficulties in producing change and thus the importance of a strong guiding coalition.... [G]uiding coalitions without strong line leadership never seem to achieve the power that is required to overcome what are often massive sources of inertia."
>
> — from *Leading Change* by John P. Kotter (Harvard Business School Press, 1996)

Some of the key players at a firm are easy to identify. They are usually managing partners or on the executive committee. Other key players may include significant rainmakers and partners who have the ability to influence the actions of the firm. On occasion, an associate or counsel of the firm might also be a key player, particularly if he or she has been advocating changes on behalf of a number of other attorneys.

Tips for Identifying Key Players

To identify key players, think back over the last several partners' meetings. Who spoke out the most and, more importantly, to whom did everyone listen? Who communicates persuasively and gathers a following? Think back also over the last several crises or difficult situations the firm has faced. Who proposed the solutions that were tried? Who took charge? Whose counsel was sought in the situation? The individuals who come to mind in answer to these questions are the ones who need to be on board from the outset.

Get the Key Players on Board

Getting the key players on board means making each one of them understand the business case for establishing a balanced hours program. One-on-one communication with the key players will probably be the most effective way to make the business case. Written materials, such as case studies of firms and businesses that have successfully created balanced hours programs and the sources listed in this book, will support the personal communication. Key players tend to be very busy, so short, focused communications should be the goal.

Frequently, a firm's key players have a long-term vision for their firm, and they will understand the need to be more competitive for top legal talent and the need to be more responsive to client concerns about attrition. They often also have their eye on their firm's bottom line. They can be expected to appreciate numbers showing the financial benefit of a balanced hours program in terms of cost savings, but they can also be expected to raise questions about overhead and firm profitability. (See Chapter 3.)

Conversation Starters

- "Our firm is losing eight associates every year, and some have been with us a while and have good relationships with our clients. Did you know that we are spending about $2,000,000 per year to replace them? We could save a lot of money if we could cut our attrition, and that is money that goes right to the bottom line."

- "Recruiting this year from the top law schools didn't go so well. Out of fifteen offers, only five were accepted. We need better recruits to maintain our profile, and you know how bad recruiting seasons seem to follow bad recruiting seasons. One thing we don't offer that a lot of recruits want is the option to work reduced schedules without penalizing their careers."

- "We've heard from several clients that they are getting fed up with the turnover of associates at our firm. We need to do something quickly to stop so many attorneys from leaving. If we can keep some associates by offering them balanced hours — the ability to cut back but not be stigmatized — we can retain our competitive edge."

- "We did a dog-and-pony show at a potential client's yesterday, and you know what they asked us? What our attrition rate was! The GC said they are taking stability and firm morale into account in choosing their outside counsel. One of their lawyers even said she had heard we have a sweatshop reputation and that we lose many lawyers every year; she asked what our action plan is for addressing the problem."

Suggested Talking Points for Key Player Conversations

- There is a direct correlation between the number of hours worked per year at a firm and attrition. Studies by The NALP Foundation and the ABA as well as several state bar associations demonstrate this. Many attorneys report leaving their firms due to the large number of hours they were expected to work, although they admit that they do not give hours as the reason when they leave because they do not want to damage their reputations.

- Law firms and corporations that have set up part-time programs in which the employees are not stigmatized for reducing their hours have saved millions of dollars a year in reduced attrition costs.

- Industry estimates are that it costs between $200,000 and $500,000 to replace one second- or third-year associate. Some of the cost items involved with replacing associates include: lost billable time by attorneys who interview recruits; increased administrative staff positions to handle the termination, recruiting, and hiring functions for the firm; lost training expenses and retraining expenses; time written off client bills for new attorneys to get up to speed; lost business that the departing attorney takes with him or her; headhunter fees; fly-back and entertaining expenses; hiring bonuses; moving and bar exam reimbursements; lost productivity.

- Associates often leave before they become profitable, and they often have to be replaced over and over again.

- A large percentage of law students report that quality of life is a major factor they consider when choosing firms. The best way to attract top law graduates is to offer them what they are looking for.

- Clients are beginning to consider firms' attrition rates when deciding which firms to hire. In addition, diversity is increasingly a major objective in hiring outside counsel. Being able to retain talented lawyers, particularly women and minorities, is becoming a business imperative.

(continued)

- Attorneys who have left firms and taken in-house counsel positions are more likely to hire firms they feel were responsive to their needs while they worked there.

- If the firm is not concerned about attrition because of a slowdown in the industry, balanced hours programs offer a way to cut payroll without losing legal talent and the relationships attorneys have built with clients.

- Allowing attorneys to reduce their schedules is part of a long-term view of the attorneys and the firm. The reduced schedule enhances loyalty, morale, productivity, and client service. Attorneys who reduce their schedules frequently return at some point in the future to a full-time schedule.

Make Balanced Hours a Priority

Firms often pursue many goals at once. Where does the creation of a balanced hours program fit into the firm's priorities? Even if everyone is on board, if the program is not given a high priority, it will not work. Part of the strategy for implementation is to communicate the urgency of getting a program in place that will stanch the flow of money and goodwill from the firm, build the firm's pool of legal talent, and meet the demands of clients for stability. Urgency creates the energy to overcome complacency and move a new program forward. One way firms can communicate urgency is to discuss frequently and with great detail the problems and potential problems caused by high turnover and the rewards that can be gained from a balanced hours program.[4] The key players will be the primary communicators.

Create the Implementation Team

A key foundation-building task is choosing the right team to develop the balanced hours program and put it into practice. The team may include the individuals who started the effort and some or all of the key players, but it will likely also include practice group heads, the head of attorney human resources, and some senior associates. Involving a cross-section of the firm provides a variety of viewpoints and smooths the path for buy-in.

---

[4] For a detailed discussion of how to create a sense of urgency in an organization, see John P. Kotter, *Leading Change* (Harvard Business School Press, 1996).

Attorneys and administrators who were instrumental in past attempts to reach goals or make changes within the firm are likely to be good choices who can be counted on to produce results.

The size of the implementation team is important. Too many individuals can stymie progress. It can be hard to get everyone together for meetings and it can take effort to keep everyone up to date on decisions, findings, and actions. Too few individuals can also be a hindrance; if there aren't enough people to do the work, progress will grind to a halt.

Personalities are an important additional consideration. Influential and active individuals are needed on the committee, but it is important to make sure that strong personalities won't clash and stall the progress. Ideally, the implementation team would include one or two individuals who are known for their diplomacy or mediation skills.

Set the Implementation Team's Mission and Course of Action

The implementation team's mission, of course, is to develop and implement a balanced hours program. The course of action may include:

- Develop a vision and goals for the balanced hours program;

- Identify the firm's problems that stem from traditional work schedules and high turnover;

- Identify potential benefits to the firm of implementing a non-stigmatized reduced hours policy;

- Communicate to the firm the reasons and the urgency for implementing the program, and communicate their support for the program;

- Develop strategies for implementing the program, including strategies for overcoming resistance;

- Take the necessary steps to implement the program and/or oversee the individuals who will have day-to-day responsibility for the implementation;

- Periodically measure the progress of the implementation and revise the implementation strategy as necessary; and

- Communicate the firm's successful steps toward its goals.

In essence, the implementation team provides the leadership that will set the course and keep the firm moving forward.

Establish a Plan

Setting the course at the outset will make implementation faster and smoother. The implementation team can set objectives for each action item, identify action items, assign work to particular members, set deadlines, and monitor progress.

Excerpt from a Sample Plan

Identify the problems caused by high turnover		
Review initial assessment work and see what needs to be updated and expanded, make recommendation	John	Due: May 7
Work with Sandy in accounting to develop hiring/attrition costs (out of pockets, bonuses, administrative salaries, etc.)	Keesha	Due: May 7
Work with Pat in billing to get hours spent in interviews, recruiting meetings, training, etc.	Maria	Due: May 7
Talk with Kirk, George, Anne, Trey, Bill, Tracey about feedback from clients and potential clients about turnover; send out e-mail to all partners re same	Peter	Due: May 7
Talk with Julia, Scott, Darrell, and Sree about recruiting last year (questions about quality of life, number of offers made and accepted with gender breakdowns for both, schools and clerkships of recruits, where our offerees went if not here)	Steve	Due: May 7

The planning process includes developing the strategy for implementation, and thus needs to address "big picture" items as well as specific tasks. The implementation team should begin thinking at this stage about how to best communicate with the firm about the program, how to combat resistance, how to overcome anticipated obstacles, how to celebrate successes, and the like. For example, the team may identify partners who are likely to oppose the program and plan ways to neutralize the opposition, or may anticipate and plan around an all-consuming firm event such as a large-scale trial that will make it hard to get the attention of the firm's attorneys. Such strategic thinking at this point will save much time and effort later.

 **Chapter Summary**

- Careful thought is required to develop a strategy for implementing a new program. Establishing a balanced hours program is not easy and requires careful planning and sustained commitment.

- Key players are the partners in managing roles and other partners who have influence at the firm. Key players are needed to sponsor the effort to develop a balanced hours program.

- Each key player needs to understand what the firm will gain from a balanced hours program. Effective techniques include talking to them one-on-one and identifying issues that are significant to the individual and to the firm.

- A crucial role for key players is understanding and communicating to others the urgency of developing a balanced hours program, which will ensure that it will be given high priority and increase the likelihood of success.

- The implementation team will develop the balanced hours policy and put it into practice. The team may include some or all of the key players, as well as a cross-section of attorneys and administrators. The ability to produce results and a team-oriented personality are important considerations in choosing team members.

- A written plan will start and maintain progress toward the goal. The plan needs to include strategies for smooth implementation as well as specific tasks.

Chapter 5

Assessing the Firm's Needs

Assessing the needs of the law firm is a crucial first step in designing a balanced hours program. Each firm needs a program that addresses its unique issues; why try to fix a broken part-time program with more technology for part-time attorneys when a bigger problem for the firm is how the firm's culture perceives part-time associates? In addition to focusing attention where it is needed most, an initial assessment also allows a firm to prioritize the items on its implementation agenda, provides the evidence needed to convince the firm that a balanced hours program is needed, and provides the firm with a benchmark against which it can measure its progress.

The benchmark is critical. If a firm learns in its initial assessment that 73% of its attorneys wish they had more time outside the office, 29% are planning to leave within three years, 46% of the associates hired three years ago have already left, and attrition costs the firm $2 million annually, the firm can measure those same areas next year and see if its efforts have reduced the numbers.

Several diagnostic tools are discussed here, each of which provides different data or gathers data in a different way. Some are quantitative, such as the statistical analyses of a firm's financial position and of the costs of attrition to the firm. Others involve qualitative assessment of the causes of dissatisfaction and attrition at the firm, and of the firm's reputation. Using several different methods will provide the most accurate picture of the firm's current position.

■ Quantitative Assessments

Firm Demographics

While most attorneys assume they know their firm's demographics, hard data can be surprising. A firm that assumes that more women than men leave the firm in child-rearing years may well find, for example, that the numbers of departures broken down by sex are not far apart if the firm's experience is similar to that of the firms surveyed by The NALP

Dickstein, Shapiro

Dickstein Shapiro Morin & Oshinsky LLP in Washington, DC, undertook an extensive self-examination that led to the conclusion that the firm needed a usable part-time policy, among other things, to stem attrition and improve attorney morale. Its deputy managing partner, Mike Nannes, has said:

> "[Leaders in the firm] recognized that, to make progress, we must first determine where we stood, and that to do that we needed to undertake an internal survey. The women lawyers elected a survey committee. This committee worked diligently in deciding what to ask and, equally important, in assuring anonymity in the responses. We retained a professional to assist us. The survey forms were distributed, responses submitted, and the results tabulated.
>
> "In the presentation detailing the survey, it became clear that there were significant differences in perceptions between men and women, partners and associates, old and young lawyers. Anecdotes were presented — eye-openers in a number of cases....
>
> "Upon analyzing the results of our survey, we recognized that many of the problems identified were not peculiar to women but related to all attorneys, perhaps with particular poignancy to those with families."

The firm's efforts have paid off. Attrition has been slowed, morale has been improved, and part-time attorneys report high levels of satisfaction. In 1999, the firm received the Constance Belfiore Quality of Life Award from the Bar Association of the District of Columbia.

Foundation.[1] Similarly, a firm that believes it has a good history of promoting women and men to partnership in equal numbers may find that only 17% of its partners are female if the firm is similar to those participating in the *NALP Directory of Legal Employers*.[2]

The following demographic data should be gathered:

- Current total number of attorneys at firm.
- Current total number of attorneys by category (equity partner, nonequity partner, of counsel, associate, contract), sex, and race.
- Number of attorneys who left the firm in the last year, by category, sex, and race.
- Number of attorneys hired by the firm in the last year, by category, sex, and race.
- Number of associates and of counsel up for partner last year, by sex, race, and schedule (full-time, part-time, other alternative schedule).
- Number of associates and of counsel promoted to partner by sex, race, and schedule (full-time, part-time, other alternative schedule).

Client Data

Taking an objective look at the information about a firm's clients can be similarly enlightening. While the demographics of in-house counsel may be interesting, additional information, such as clients' diversity objectives and longevity with the firm, is vitally important. Information to gather includes:

- Current number of unique clients of the firm.
- Current number of unique matters the firm is handling for each client.
- Revenue received from each unique client in the past year.
- Number of new clients who retained the firm in the past year.
- Number of clients who discontinued the firm's services last year.
- For each of the clients serviced in the past year, a statement of the client's diversity objectives, if known.

---

[1] See The NALP Foundation for Law Career Research and Education, *Keeping The Keepers: Strategies for Associate Retention in Times of Attrition* (1998) (for the period 1988 to 1996, an average of 43% of associates left their firms within three years of hire; approximately 41% of male associates left, and 45% of the female associates left in that time period).

[2] NALP Research, "Women and Attorneys of Color at Law Firms — 2003" (based on firms submitting data for the *NALP Directory of Legal Employers* and available online at www.nalp.org/nalpresearch/mw03sum.htm).

Recruiting Data

Law firms sell legal talent, and successful recruiting of top-notch legal talent is essential to a firm's reputation, longevity, and profitability. To assess the current state of a firm's recruiting program, the following data should be collected:

- Total number of new hires in the past year, by category, sex, and race.
- Breakdown of the total number of new hires by attorneys hired as part of planned firm growth and attorneys hired to replace attorneys who had left.
- Total number of offers made, by category, sex, and race.
- The number of new hires who attended a prestigious law school or joined the firm from a judicial clerkship, or, for lateral hires, who came to the firm from prestigious former employment.
- For each offeree who did not accept the firm's offer, the employment the offeree accepted, if known.

Competitive Data

Law firms compete with one another for legal talent and clients. Where a firm stands in relation to its peer firms is part of the assessment picture. Identify several firms that are considered competitors of the firm (more in an urban area), and gather data for the firm and its competitors in the following areas:

- Reputation for intensity of attorney work schedules (e.g., sweatshop versus relaxed atmosphere).
- Alternative work arrangements offered, including policy regarding effect on salary, benefits, bonuses, and advancement, if known.
- Total number of attorneys working alternative schedules.
- Total number of partners working alternative schedules.
- Awards, honors, and favorable press coverage for quality of life, work/life balance, or alternative work schedules.
- Number of recruits who chose competitor firms over your firm.
- Number of clients or potential clients who chose competitor firms over your firm.

Financial Data

A chief goal of a balanced hours program is to increase the profitability of a law firm over the long term. An assessment of current revenue and costs will be an important benchmark when evaluating the success of a balanced hours program and, in the shorter term, may be instrumental in convincing attorneys in the firm of the need for a balanced hours program. Financial data to gather include total revenue, expenses, and profit for the prior year.

Attrition Costs

Industry estimates state that firms lose between $250,000 and $500,000 every time they have to replace a second- or third-year associate. The elements of the costs were listed in Chapter 1; they include administrative expenses, out-of-pocket expenses, and time-related expenses. Knowing a firm's costs of lost resources, recruiting, and retraining as precisely as possible is important to be able to demonstrate tangibly the financial benefits the firm will receive from reduced attrition.

To calculate attrition-related costs, calculate such things as the amount of money the firm spends on administrative personnel who oversee recruiting and training of new attorneys and who process paperwork for new hires and departures, and multiply by the amount of time spent on such activities. Adding up the out-of-pocket items is not so difficult; the firm's accounting department probably already tracks interviewing lunches and fly-back airfares by a recruiting code. At most firms, calculating the time spent by attorneys wooing and interviewing candidates and training new attorneys is captured on timesheets and is also easily calculated.

A worksheet is provided in the appendix to consolidate this type of information.

■ PAR Usability Test

Every firm with a part-time policy in place should take the PAR Usability Test. (See pages 31–37.) The resulting information will respond in part to the question sure to be asked: Why does the firm need a balanced hours program if it already has a part-time policy?

■ Qualitative Assessment

To get a more complete picture of the firm's needs for change, a firm must know what its attorneys, clients, and recruits are thinking and feeling about the firm. This section includes some suggestions for seeking out and recording anecdotal evidence about these issues.

What Are the Firm's Attorneys Thinking?

As discussed in Chapter 2, attorneys are reluctant to tell their firms their real feelings; the risks of being viewed as whiny and unprofessional are too high. For this reason, outside consultants who can guarantee respondents' anonymity and who can make attorneys feel more comfortable about self-disclosing will have the most success in obtaining valid responses. Outside consultants are discussed in the next section.

If a firm is unwilling to hire outside consultants, it can use questionnaires, conduct one-on-one interviews, and survey former employees. Some suggestions follow, but be forewarned that the responses may not be as accurate, reliable, or complete.

Questionnaires. Questionnaires have the advantage of anonymity, but have the disadvantage of low response rates and lack of ability to seek further information regarding responses. In developing a questionnaire, a firm should be sure to include an introductory paragraph about the purpose of the questionnaire, confidentiality, and the importance of honest responses. Also, initially, the questionnaire should ask for some demographic information that will help interpret the responses but not identify individuals by name (e.g., level within firm, such as partner or associate; length of time with firm by range, such as 0–2 years).

The questionnaire should solicit opinions about morale at the firm, feelings about work hours and workloads, reasons for attrition, predictions of future attrition, and suggestions for improvement. A mixture of multiple choice and open-ended questions is generally most effective. Questions should be phrased as neutrally as possible. Keep the questionnaire short to maximize the response rate and provide instructions for returning the response in a way that will preserve confidentiality.

A sample questionnaire is provided in the appendix.

Interviews. While interviews may not provide complete or accurate information because of attorneys' reluctance to voice schedule-related concerns, they may nevertheless provide some insights if conducted in such a manner as to inspire trust and openness. Getting usable information depends largely on a firm's choice of interviewers. Partners who are known for their approachability and are interested in issues of work/life balance may be good choices. Each could be asked to interview several attorneys with whom he or she has an established relationship. A member of the implementation team should keep a list of the attorneys who will be interviewed and make an effort to have the group of interviewees be as diverse as possible. If using the initial group of interviewers will not result in a sufficient number of attorneys being interviewed or will not provide a diverse enough pool of interviewees, other highly placed partners should be drafted for the effort. The more people who are involved as interviewers, however, the harder it is to maintain confidentiality and consistency.

A written script or list of questions will help ensure that the main issues are covered in each interview. During the interview, the purpose of the interview should be discussed and confidentiality should be assured to the extent it is possible. Written summaries of the interviews, without the interviewees' names, should be prepared and compiled.

Clearly, interviews are a very time-consuming exercise. If the firm decides that the interviews should be conducted by its attorneys, it should take into consideration that time spent interviewing means less time available for billable work, and that the interview process will likely proceed slowly because of the attorneys' obligations to attend to client needs. For these reasons, and because of the uncertain usability of interview results when conducted by members of the firm, the use of outside consultants is preferable.

Survey of alumni. If a firm wants to know why attorneys leave, the most logical source of information is the departed attorneys themselves. Tracking them down, getting them to respond, and obtaining truthful answers to questions about their departures may all prove difficult. A firm is likely to have more success if a personnel administrator rather than an attorney makes personal phone calls to the firm's departed attorneys and conducts an interview with promises of confidentiality. The departed attorneys may be reluctant to state anything other than neutral platitudes ("I left to pursue a better opportunity," "I've always wanted to teach," "I wanted to try government work for a while"), but if they are told that many attorneys are being called in an effort to identify areas in which the firm could improve and that their names and current positions will be kept separate from their responses, they may be more forthcoming. As with interviews of attorneys who are currently employed by the firm, a written script and written summaries of responses are necessary.

Outside consultants. The best picture of a firm may well come from the use of outside consultants. In addition to having the necessary detachment and expertise in getting information from their subjects, experienced consultants also have the benefit of perspective: They have presumably worked with other similarly situated firms and can provide an idea of how the firm compares to others.

Finding a consultant with the right expertise can be a challenge. Look for consultants who have experience with informational interviews and questionnaires, and also who have worked with law firms of similar size before. Word of mouth, Internet searches, and consultant directories will provide a starting point. Interview potential consultants in depth to find the right fit for the firm. Questions to ask potential consultants, in addition to experience and cost, include how they propose to assess the firm's needs for change, how they plan to preserve confidentiality, the length of time they estimate it will take to complete the project, and the format of their end product.

One implementation team member should be appointed to act as liaison between the firm and the consultant. This controls costs and cuts the risk of miscommunication due to conflicting directions. This team member will need to explain to the firm's attorneys who the consultants are and why they have been hired, and encourage cooperation from the attorneys.

What Are the Firm's Clients Thinking?

Additional evidence about what the firm needs to change may well come from its clients. Some law firms regularly survey their clients to see how they can improve their performance, whether through written questionnaires, phone interviews, or in-person meetings. It would not be difficult to include in these client surveys questions relating to attrition, which will tell the firms whether turnover is damaging their client relationships or keeping them from winning new business.

If a firm is reluctant to ask questions directly, it may be able to gather enough anecdotal evidence to tell if its clients perceive a problem. Ask the attorneys in the firm to report any situations in which clients have mentioned attrition. Also ask for reports of instances in which clients have raised the issue of attrition indirectly, such as complaints about the loss of relationships or institutional knowledge when an attorney left the firm, requests for more diversity in the team of attorneys working for the client, or refusals to pay for time spent getting new attorneys up to speed on the matters the firm is handling for the client. Similarly, ask attorneys who have recently obtained or tried to obtain new business whether they have heard concerns about attrition or diversity from prospects. Compile the responses and see if they provide evidence that client relationships will improve with increased retention.

What Are the Firm's Recruits Thinking?

The ability to attract high-quality talent is important to all firms, and a firm's reputation largely determines how able it is to get the talent it needs. Law school students, law clerks, and others looking for a law firm position research quality of life intensely, and studies show that they want to work at firms where they can balance their lives.[3] Compiling evidence of a firm's reputation and the desires of the types of attorneys it hopes to attract will show if providing a balanced hours program will improve its recruiting chances.

Ask the firm's recruiters and attorneys who interview candidates what types of questions or concerns candidates raise with respect to hours or quality of life. When added to

---

[3] Deborah L. Rhode, "Balanced Lives: Changing the Culture of Legal Practice," ABA Commission on Women in the Profession (2001) at 15; Kirstin Downey Grimsley, "Family a Priority for Young Workers; Survey Finds Change in Men's Thinking," *The Washington Post*, May 3, 2000 at E1; Catalyst, *Advancing Women in Business — The Catalyst Guide* 26 (1998).

the objective data already collected, the firm will see whether it has an adequate pool to draw from, how desirable recruits consider the firm, and whether the firm can attract and hire a diverse group. Collect media reports of quality of life at the firm, including associate and summer associate surveys conducted by American Lawyer Media and comments about the firm on Internet sites (e.g., Vault.com, Findlaw.com Career Center, pardc.org).

What Is Being Said …

Here are some comments available for public viewing on the Internet:

- "I am currently a part-time attorney at [name of firm deleted] and really believe this is one of the best firms in the country at which a mother can practice law. There are a number of part-time women attorneys in our office. There is no one part-time 'track.' Each of us has worked out the schedule that works for us and the firm. There have been women who took leaves of absence, worked part-time, and then went on to make partner. Also, I am aware of at least one father who opted to work part-time for family reasons."

- "I am a white male.... During my years at [firm], I have never seen a part-time attorney (usually a mother and occasionally a father) make partner. Asking for part-time and other 'mother' (or 'father') perks is CAREER SUICIDE at [firm]. Really. None of the current female partners (that is, the VERY few that exist at [firm], especially in the corporate group, which hands-down wields the most political power at [firm]) are or were part-time."

- "[E]veryone will have their own experience no doubt, but I felt that it was all hype about family atmosphere and was not a friendly place except for the staff.... And forget work-at-home days, because the partners want to see you in the office and even check to see if you are there in the evening."

In addition, Vault.com lists the 20 best law firms to work at based on quality of life, PARDC.org provides information about the best firms in the District of Columbia for part-time work, and several bar associations present awards to firms that have good quality-of-life programs.

 **Chapter Summary**

→ Assessing the firm's current position, objectively and subjectively, helps to focus its efforts on the areas that need to be addressed and provides a baseline against which the firm can measure its progress.

→ Objective, demographic information about the firm's attorneys, clients, recruits, and competitors is important.

→ The subjective, qualitative assessment focuses on what the firm's attorneys, clients, and recruits think of the firm. The firm can survey and interview its attorneys but would likely get more accurate results if it used an outside consultant. Consultants can also survey clients, or the firm can compile anecdotal evidence.

→ Recruits pay attention to firms' reputations. Accurately assessing how the firm is perceived is important.

Chapter 6

Creating a Balanced Hours Policy

A well-designed policy, tailored to meet a firm's specific needs, is the cornerstone of a balanced hours program. Although one could certainly ask friends for copies of their firms' policies or use the model policy that is provided in the appendix, a unique policy that a firm can comfortably adopt is the best approach. Taking the time to reflect on a firm's particular business objectives and culture and drafting a policy suitable to both is an exercise that will pay large dividends.

■ Process

Drafting by a large committee can be tedious. Therefore, the implementation team may want to appoint a subgroup to create the initial draft. Having several points of view is helpful, so a drafting group ideally should include at least one associate, partner, and administrator. It is important that some of the people in the drafting group be persons who will potentially be affected by the policy; for example, an attorney who has expressed interest in reducing hours and an attorney who supervises other attorneys both have valuable perspectives to offer.

In its initial planning stages, the implementation team will have decided how to proceed once an initial draft has been created. One approach would be for the team as a whole to review the draft and suggest revisions and then circulate a revised draft to the attorneys earlier identified as "key players" for comments. Whether the policy should then be formally adopted by the management committee or other appropriate entity or first be circulated to the firm's attorneys at large for comments prior to adoption depends on the firm's culture and the strategy created by the implementation team.

■ Fundamental Principles

While creating the policy, the drafting subcommittee should keep in mind the basic principles of proportionality and flexibility.

Proportionality is fundamental to a non-stigmatized policy. Without proportionality, perceptions of unfairness will undermine success. Not only do pay, benefits, and

Why Have a Written Policy?

Until recent years, most current part-time programs were unwritten. The programs tended to be ad hoc; highly valued attorneys who wanted to reduce their hours were permitted to do so — sometimes on the condition that they not disclose the terms of their arrangement — while others were left out in the cold. Attorneys at firms with unwritten policies were unsure if a part-time policy existed or, if they did know it existed, what its terms were. At some firms, women attorneys knew the terms of the part-time policy, but men attorneys did not.

It is now more commonplace for part-time policies to be recorded in writing, but many written policies are deliberately vague. Compensation, advancement, and other key issues are left to the individual attorney to negotiate with management. While firms with vague policies may be trying to achieve flexibility in responding to individual circumstances, they are setting themselves up for problems. Without specific guidelines, attorneys and their supervisors are left to make things up as they go along. Inevitably, attorneys will perceive that they are being treated differently. In addition to breeding unfairness and poor morale, the uneven application of policies is a discrimination suit waiting to happen.

A specific, written policy is essential to a balanced hours program. As human resources professionals will confirm, written policies establish the intent of management, eliminate confusion, and foster uniform treatment of employees by guiding supervisors. A written policy also lets a firm know that management "means it" when it says lawyers can reduce their hours under certain circumstances.

bonuses need to be proportional, but so do billable hour requirements, assignments, and advancement.

Flexibility is also fundamental. For any program to work, it has to address an actual problem in a meaningful way. Balanced hours programs have to be flexible enough to accommodate the needs of individual attorneys in order to allow attorneys to find balance in their lives; requiring attorneys who want to cut their hours to work four days a week will not address the needs of attorneys who want to work fewer hours per day or fewer months in the year. Similarly, a policy that limits the length of time an attorney can work reduced hours — for example, that requires attorneys to return to full-time work after six months or a year — will not retain valuable attorneys who are looking for balance over the long term.

Essential Elements of a Balanced Hours Program

A written policy should specify the following:

- Eligibility for balanced hours schedules.
- Process for requesting balanced hours.
- Guidelines for creating balanced schedules.
- Compensation, including benefits and bonus.
- Guidelines for creating written work expectations for the balanced hours attorney.
- Assignment process, including nonbillable work.
- Effect on advancement.
- Compensation for additional hours worked and a mechanism for preventing frequent excess hours.
- An agreement in writing.
- Training for the supervisor and balanced hours attorney.
- The process in case of emergencies.
- Periodic review of schedule.

Eligibility for Balanced Hours Schedules

The policy should state at the outset who is eligible to work a balanced schedule. Is it all attorneys? Only associates? Only attorneys who have been with the firm a minimum amount of time?

The best policies are those that allow all attorneys to work balanced hours regardless of their reason for wanting to do so. A broad definition of applicability will attract and retain different types of valuable attorneys, from a former Supreme Court clerk who wants to train for a marathon to a former Executive Branch official who has a health condition. A mistake that many firms still make is limiting reduced hours schedules to attorneys who are mothers of young children; this not only limits the type of attorney the work option will attract and retain but also runs the serious risk of creating a stigmatized "mommy track" that will not advance the firm's interests to any appreciable extent.

Additionally, a broad definition of eligibility is a pre-emptive strike against backlash. The media have reported in recent years that nonparents often feel resentful of parents who are allowed to reduce their hours. While we discuss managing backlash in greater detail in Chapter 9, it is worth noting at this juncture that giving everyone the choice of working a balanced hours or a standard hours schedule goes a long way toward eliminating resentment.

It follows from this that employers should avoid asking attorneys about the reason they prefer a balanced hours schedule. To quote one panel of human resources professionals, employers need to ask not "why do you need it?," but "will it work?"[1] In the corporate world, successful work/life programs provide reduced hours to all employees, or entire categories of employees, without regard to the reason a reduced schedule is sought. A good example is Fannie Mae, where the focus of inquiry is on the business case — that is, on how the employee will get his or her work done — and the reason for seeking an alternative work schedule is never asked.[2]

Should attorneys have to be at the firm a minimum amount of time before seeking a balanced hours schedule? Ideally, the answer should be no; firms should make balanced hours schedules available to new hires. Balanced hours policies will have the greatest impact on a firm's recruiting efforts if the firm hires attorneys who want to work reduced hours from the outset.

---

[1] Williams, *Unbending Gender*, at 98.
[2] Presentation by Susan Holik, then Vice President for Human Resources, Fannie Mae, at "Redefining the Life of a Lawyer" (District of Columbia Bar Association Winter Convention, March 2, 1999).

Although it is not uncommon for firms to require attorneys to be employed by the firm for a minimum amount of time (usually a year or two) before submitting a proposal to reduce their schedules, more firms have begun to hire attorneys on a balanced hours basis. Information from legal search consultants and law school career services professionals indicates that the number of applicants who want balanced hours schedules is growing. Making reduced hours available to new hires allows firms to tap this labor pool.

Process for Requesting Balanced Hours

What does an attorney have to do to request a balanced hours schedule? Who approves the schedule?

An established procedure for requesting a balanced hours schedule will ensure a fair, even-handed approval process and eliminate the sense that balanced hours are available only ad hoc or only to favorite sons and daughters. The procedure should include: a request made in writing by the attorney; a written proposal stating how the attorney's work would get done and how the schedule would work; a timeframe for making a request; a discussion with a balanced hours coordinator,[3] mentor, or role model; a meeting with a supervising attorney or practice head; modification of the proposal, if necessary; the title of the person or committee making the decision whether to approve the request; a process for appealing a denial; and a safety valve to shortcut the process in the case of an emergency.

The process for requesting balanced hours should be specific — not only to impart a sense of fairness and predictability in how schedule requests are approved but also to provide a framework for thinking through how an individual attorney's requested balanced schedule would work. A terrific example of process exists at Deloitte Touche Tohmatsu; Deloitte has developed an interactive process on CD for its employees to use in deciding whether to make a request, what to request, and how to develop a proposal for meeting the employer's business needs.

A questionnaire that a prospective balanced hours attorney could fill out would also be beneficial. The attorney, after thinking through the details of his or her request, would share the answers to the questionnaire with a balanced hours coordinator or mentor and with his or her supervisor as part of the approval process. Modifications would be made as necessary. A list of suggested items the attorney should think through is provided in Chapter 9.

---

[3] See Chapter 8 for a discussion of balanced hours coordinators.

Guidelines for Creating Reduced Schedules

Creating a policy that is universally applicable does not mean creating a policy that is one-size-fits-all. Attorneys have different work and personal needs, and some may need to work fewer hours each day, or each week, or each year. Policies should be flexible enough to allow for individuation.

Here are some balanced hours schedules that have worked well at law firms:

1. **Fewer hours each day.** Attorneys agree to work a set number of hours per day with regular beginning and ending times.

2. **Fewer hours each week.** Attorneys agree to work a set number of hours per week but have flexibility in determining the hours they will be in the office. For example, an attorney might work from 9:00 am to 5:00 pm on Monday, work from 9:00 am to 2:00 pm on Tuesday and take a sick parent to the doctor, and then work from 9:00 am to 3:00 pm on the remaining days of the week. The following week, the schedule may vary.

3. **Fewer hours each year.** Attorneys agree to work set amounts of billable and nonbillable hours over the course of a year. This works well for litigators and others with unpredictable schedules. An attorney on this type of schedule may work 70- or 80-hour work weeks while in trial, and then take time off or work 20-hour work weeks when not busy. *Caveat:* The firm and the attorney need to make sure that compensatory time off is taken; this is discussed more in later sections of this chapter.

Balanced hours schedules also need to be flexible in terms of duration. While many attorneys want reduced hours for a short period of time or a defined longer period of time, others may want them indefinitely. Some firms, however, set deadlines requiring balanced hours attorneys to return to standard schedules after a year or two, or before being considered for partner. Allowing indefinite balanced hours schedules, subject to periodic reviews as discussed in this chapter, is the best way to support attorneys' needs.

An important component of this flexibility is allowing attorneys to move between balanced hours and standard hours without fear of repercussion. Research shows the value of recognizing the trend toward "phased careers" and allowing variation in employment schedules without career penalty.[4] As attorneys grow and mature and face different challenges and desires in their lives inside and outside the office, their schedule-related needs

---

[4] Phyllis Moen and Yan Yu, "Having it All: Overall Work/Life Success in Two-Earner Families." 7 *Research in Sociology of Work* (1999) 109, 132.

will change. Attorneys who have reduced their hours may wish to return to standard hours to work on a particular project or for an indefinite period of time. Attorneys who have been working fewer hours per day may want to change to work fewer hours per week. Attorneys may wish to move between balanced and standard hours several times over the course of their careers.

Compensation Including Benefits and Bonus

It used to be common, until the late 1990s, for part-time attorneys to "take a haircut" — that is, to work a percentage of a full-time schedule and get paid a smaller percentage of a full-time salary. A typical example of the haircut was an arrangement where an attorney worked 80% of full-time hours and got paid 60% of full-time pay. Firms with such arrangements justified them on the mistaken belief that overhead costs were higher for part-time attorneys. (This belief is discussed in detail in Chapter 3.)

Proportional pay for proportional work is essential to a successful balanced hours program. An 80% schedule should yield an 80% paycheck. Providing less than proportional pay penalizes reduced hours work and will quickly undermine a balanced hours program, and it may set the firm up for an equal pay act lawsuit if the attorneys who have reduced their hours for less than proportional pay are women who are doing the same work as men for less money.

Benefits. For the same reasons, benefits that are at least proportional should be provided. Historically, some firms eliminate all benefits entirely for part-time attorneys, but it is more common nowadays for firms to provide full or proportional benefits.

Most firms provide "insurance" benefits and "time" benefits for their attorneys. The "insurance" benefits include such things as medical, dental, vision, life, and disability insurance. Typically, firms pay the full cost for their standard hours attorneys. Many pay the full cost for their balanced hours attorneys as well, although some pay only a proportional amount for balanced hours attorneys. While this practice conforms to the principle of proportionality, it is important to make sure it does not act as a deterrent to reducing hours.

One issue that arises with insurance benefits is whether balanced hours attorneys remain eligible for insurance under the firm's insurance policies if the policies require a minimum number of hours to be worked each week for eligibility. One way some firms have addressed the minimum-hours-per-week issue is to look at all the hours a balanced hours attorney works, not just billable hours. Thus, time spent talking to clients from home, working on business development, or doing pro bono work would be counted toward the weekly minimum hour requirement. Additionally, policies can be examined to see if they permit averaging of hours to meet the minimum weekly amount.

"Time" benefits include vacation and other leave plans. Typically, these are calculated and awarded proportionally to the schedule worked. Thus, an attorney who is working 80% of a standard schedule at a firm that gives associates three weeks of vacation per year would still get three weeks of vacation, but his or her pay for those weeks would be 80% of the standard pay rate.

Other benefits, such as profit sharing, retirement plans, cafeteria plans, and the like, should remain available to balanced hours attorneys, on a pro-rated basis if reasonable.

Bonuses. Bonuses are given to attorneys to recognize exceptional work, motivate business development, reward high numbers of billable hours, bring individual attorneys' income into line with that of colleagues, retain good attorneys, and for other reasons. At some firms, the amount of bonuses is significant — up to $50,000 — and represents a substantial portion of an attorney's income.[5] Balanced hours attorneys should remain eligible to receive bonuses according to the same criteria as standard hours attorneys, and their eligibility and their bonuses should be adjusted on a pro-rated basis in accordance with their reduced hours.

Ineligibility for bonuses, either due to a formal policy or due to practice, contributes to the stigma of a balanced hours schedule. Moreover, as with salary, bonuses send messages to individual attorneys about how their performance is valued and what their future is with the firm. A policy or practice that makes balanced hours attorneys ineligible for bonuses promotes attrition.

Firms that maintain balanced hours attorneys' eligibility for bonuses emphasize factors other than, or in addition to, hours worked. They apply eligibility criteria and award bonus amounts on a pro-rated basis. For example, if a bonus criterion at a particular firm is meeting the firm's target billable hours requirement, balanced hours attorneys would be eligible for a bonus if they met their individual billable hours targets, and the amount of bonus they receive would be in proportion to the percentage schedule they are working (e.g., an attorney working an 80% schedule would receive 80% of the bonus paid to standard hours attorneys who achieve the billable hours target). This pro-rated bonus structure works whether an attorney works a reduced number of hours per week or per year.

Guidelines for Creating Written Work Expectations for the Balanced Hours Attorney

A key component of a balanced hours policy is the number of hours an attorney should work. Where a firm has established a billable hours requirement or target for standard hours attorneys, that figure can be used to establish a proportional billable hours target for balanced hours attorneys. At firms with no billable hours requirement or target, a balanced hours attorney can average his or her typical billable hours while on a full-time

---

[5] Bryan Rund and Bill Kisliuk, "D.C. Salary Watch," *Legal Times*, Sept. 11, 2000, available on http://www.law.com/special/professionals/timeline1.html.

schedule to arrive at what "standard" hours are for him or her and then set a proportional number of hours to bill while on a balanced schedule.

Of course, attorneys do more than bill hours. They participate in bar activities, serve on firm committees, perform pro bono work, develop business, take continuing legal education courses, and the like. It is therefore important for the balanced hours policy to require attorneys to include both billable and nonbillable hours in the attorney's proposal for a balanced hours schedule.

Policies that do not recognize the need for nonbillable time are setting balanced hours attorneys up for failure over the long term. Attorneys, understandably wanting to maximize billable time, plan to use every available work hour for billable client work. They then struggle to fit firm administrative work and professional development activities into their non-working hours, and many admit they have given up altogether on business development, firm management, and pro bono work. While they justify the trade-off as "worth it" so they can have more time outside the office, ignoring such nonbillable work can irreversibly hurt attorneys' professional development and partnership chances.

The work expectations portion of the policy should also discuss what the balanced hours attorney's workload will be. As discussed in Chapter 2, a frequent complaint heard from lawyers at law firms is that part-time attorneys find their schedules gradually increasing back to full-time. *Schedule creep is almost always caused by the failure to adjust the balanced hours attorney's caseload to match the shorter work hours.* Often there is an unspoken expectation on the part of the firm that the attorney will continue to do the same amount of work — and a corresponding desire on the part of the attorney to prove that he or she is still a valuable team member who can pull his or her own weight. Including workload management in the balanced hours policy will require the firm to examine the reasonableness of its expectation and prevent the well-intentioned attorney from inadvertently self-sabotaging a balanced hours schedule.

Work assignment systems vary greatly among firms and even within firms, requiring individually tailored work management policies. The ideal is to have a flexible policy that encourages discussion between balanced hours attorneys and their supervisors about the workloads feasible within reduced-hours schedules; the policy should also provide guidelines for distribution of work. Cutting back on the number of clients is an approach that has worked well for some balanced hours attorneys. This allows attorneys to sustain meaningful contact with their remaining clients and to maintain the same type of practice they had as standard hours attorneys.

Where it is not possible to cut back on the number of clients, cutting back on the number of matters often will

> *Caveat:* While the balanced hours attorney should not expect to be able to cherry pick his or her assignments, the supervisor should be alert to ensure that the balanced hours attorney is not punished for reducing hours through loss of all desirable assignments or clients.

allow a manageable workload. This approach may well be optimal for an attorney who typically works for only one or two clients and for those who handle a large number of routine matters.

Assignment Process, Including Nonbillable Work

How much success and job satisfaction attorneys experience often depends on the type of work they do. A chief complaint from attorneys working part-time is that once they reduced their hours, they began to get less interesting work. Some are even removed from their chosen area of practice altogether. Tales of relegation to document reviews and repetitive administrative work are not uncommon. Not surprisingly, attorneys in such situations often feel disrespected and leave their firms.

Even if balanced hours attorneys whose work assignments suffer from their reduction in hours do not leave their firms, their development as attorneys will suffer. If litigation associates, for example, are not given the opportunity to take depositions or argue motions, their skills will not progress and they will not be judged ready when it is time to be considered for partnership.

Decentralized work assignment practices are common at law firms. Similar to what is called "'Hey, you' tasking" in military circles, it typically involves a partner assigning work to the first person he or she sees after a need for work arises. Clearly, a physical presence at the firm is necessary to obtain work under such systems, and the more time one is present, the more likely one is to get interesting assignments. To ensure that balanced hours attorneys receive appropriate assignments, it may be necessary for the balanced hours policy to address how work is assigned at the firm. As a corollary, the firm may want to put an assignment review procedure in place to make sure that balanced hours attorneys are receiving challenging and interesting work.

> After a task force at Deloitte Touche Tohmatsu found that one of the most significant career obstacles for women was the system under which assignments were made, the firm began a system of reviewing assignments periodically to ensure that men and women were given equal access to desirable assignments.

Assignment to firm committees and other nonbillable firm work is also important. Often, balanced hours attorneys find that they are shut out of firm committees and management, usually as the result of well-meaning attempts to reduce the attorneys' workloads. Assignments to firm committees should be periodically reviewed to make sure that balanced hours attorneys are included.

Effect on Advancement

Do balanced hours associates and counsel remain on partnership track? Is their advancement delayed and, if so, when and by how much?

Some firms still take attorneys with reduced hours off the partnership track, either formally or de facto. Of course, such a practice makes reducing hours a professional kiss of death for the attorney — and is also the kiss of death for a balanced hours program. There is no need to remove balanced hours attorneys from the partnership track as long as the partnership decision is based on factors such as ability, experience, and potential rather than strictly on the number of hours worked.

It may be necessary for a firm to articulate its criteria for partnership at the same time that it drafts its balanced hours policy. Some suggested criteria and comments on how they relate to balanced hours attorneys:

- One criterion for partnership may be a certain level of professional maturity and confidence. Assuming balanced hours attorneys are not given less desirable assignments, they should develop these skills as do other attorneys, although perhaps on a more extended schedule.

- Another criterion may be that a lawyer has "paid his or her dues." Balanced schedule attorneys pay the same "dues" as other attorneys — they just pay them on a different schedule.

- A third criterion may be business development potential. Assuming that balanced hours attorneys have an arrangement that includes nonbillable as well as billable hours, they should become equally adept not only at "doing the work," but also at "getting the work" through time invested in bar associations, firm committees, and client development.

Advancement opportunities should be at least proportional. This can be achieved in several ways. Some firms take into consideration at what point in their careers associates reduce their schedules; if the associates have worked for five or six years full-time, then reducing their hours by 20% or 30% for a couple of years may not affect the time at which they are considered for partnership. Other firms do not consider hours worked in determining readiness for partnership but rather focus on skills, experience, and potential to attract clients; at such firms, part-time associates are considered at the same time as their full-time counterparts. Both of these examples show advancement that is more than proportional. An example of proportional advancement would be a case where an attorney who worked full-time for four years and then reduced to half-time would be considered for partnership after twelve years in a firm with an eight-year partnership track. A more typical example, again for a firm with an eight-year track, is an associate who works full-time for four years and then moves to an 80% schedule; that associate would be considered for partnership after nine years (every five years on an 80% schedule would slow advancement by one year).

Compensation for Additional Hours Worked and a Mechanism for Preventing Frequent Excess Hours

Inevitably, there will be times when a balanced hours attorney will have to work during a time when he or she is not scheduled to work. Will this additional time be compensated and, if so, will it be compensated with money or comp time?

Firms have approached this issue in different ways. Some do not compensate for any extra time worked. If an attorney who has reduced his or her hours works a significant amount of overtime, such as five or more hours per week on a regular basis, the failure to compensate for the additional time will prevent the balanced hours program from achieving its intended results. The attorneys who have cut their hours will feel cheated and other attorneys in the firm will view the situation as evidence that the balanced hours program is not viable; moreover, if the attorney who is working extra uncompensated hours is female, an Equal Pay Act suit could result.

Some firms pay reduced hours attorneys for extra time worked on an hourly basis or according to an established formula, or through an end-of-year bonus. Others pay reduced hour attorneys for all extra hours worked over a particular threshold. For example, one firm pays its reduced hours attorneys for all hours they work in excess of 10% of their annual agreement.

While it is preferable to recognize the extra efforts of reduced hours attorneys with additional compensation than not to recognize overtime, attorneys who have reduced their hours want time and not money. A better arrangement would provide attorneys with compensatory time off close to the extra time they worked (and monetary compensation if the attorney is not able to use compensatory time). All too often, attorneys at firms that allow compensatory time but do not encourage or require that it be used within a certain period of time find that they are unable to use the compensatory time.

The best policy is to work to eliminate significant extra hours in the first place. Workload management and prevention of supervisory tactics that undermine balanced schedules both contribute to maintaining the schedule the firm has agreed to provide to an attorney. One firm surveyed by PAR in 2001 expressed surprise at being asked how it compensated attorneys for extra hours; the firm's balanced hours attorneys did not work more than the hours they had agreed to. A mechanism was in place for the part-time coordinator to troubleshoot schedule issues that could lead to extra hours, but this mechanism, which included direct conversations with partners who assigned too much work to a part-time attorney, did not have to be used. This firm has one of the most successful balanced hours programs in the country.

A written policy that provides (1) comp time to be taken within several months of extra work hours and (2) monetary compensation provided as a back-up if comp time cannot be taken and that is supported by management polices preventing regular episodes of extra work will prevent schedule creep and lead to a profitable balanced hours program.

Troubleshooting Schedule Creep

- **Monitor for schedule creep:** Watch the hours of balanced attorneys on a monthly basis. Expect fluctuations, but if a balanced hours attorney's hours are consistently higher than budgeted, suspect schedule creep.

- **Investigate:** Ask the attorney and his or her supervisor the reason for the excess hours. Ensure that the supervisor is not assigning the balanced hours attorney duties that are inconsistent with his or her schedule.

- **Remedy:** Remind the supervisor of the business reasons for having a balanced hours program, redesign or reassign work to prevent the creep, and encourage the attorney to take comp time.

Recording the Arrangement in Writing

The balanced hours policy should require that the balanced hours attorney and his or her supervisor reduce to writing their agreements regarding the balanced hours schedule. A written document will provide certainty and a basis for evaluating whether the arrangement is working. The firm may want to provide a checklist or short-answer form for the supervisor and attorney to use.

Training for the Supervisor and Balanced Hours Attorney

As smart as they are, attorneys and their supervising attorneys cannot know everything instinctively. The firm needs to teach balanced hours attorneys and their supervisors how to manage their expectations, ensure excellent client service, address schedule-related issues, strengthen communication, use technology to be more productive, and the like. Training is discussed in greater detail in the next chapter, and the written policy should include that balanced hours attorneys and their supervisors are required to take the training the firm decides to offer.

Emergencies

Emergencies will arise inside and outside the office. Giving some consideration at the outset to how the firm expects the balanced hours attorney to respond to emergencies is a good idea. Should the attorney have certain technology and access to information at home in order to be able to address problems without having to come in to the office? Should the attorney have a colleague at the firm who can act as a back-up if necessary?

Periodic Review of Schedule

Things do not get done unless they are scheduled, and evaluation of how a balanced hours schedule is working is too important to leave to chance. While the hope would be that balanced hours attorneys and their supervisors would talk on a regular basis about how the arrangement is going, the realities of fast-paced practice and disinclinations to confront negative situations often prevent such ongoing communication. The policy, therefore, should include periodic reviews of the balanced hours arrangement. Frequent evaluations are suggested initially — perhaps every two to three months — moving to evaluations every six to twelve months as the arrangement matures. The supervisor and attorney should be involved in the review; additional involvement by the balanced hours coordinator (see Chapter 9), the department head, and others may also be desirable. Topics to include in the review are whether work is being completed in a timely fashion, whether the attorney is being responsive to clients, whether the agreed upon schedule is being adhered to, and whether there are ways for the attorney to be more productive through use of technology or delegation. If modifications to the balanced hours arrangement are necessary after a review, they should be put in writing. A bit of extra work in the early stages to nip problems in the bud is far preferable to suffering silently with an unacceptable situation.

Tips for Conducting Reviews

A model for reviews that may be beneficial is one in which the attorney's schedule is reviewed by his or her supervising attorney at the same time that he or she is given a performance evaluation, and then reviewed again six months later by the balanced hours coordinator with input from the supervisor.

It may be helpful for supervisors and attorneys to have a form to fill out or a list of questions to answer when reviewing the effectiveness of balanced hours schedules to ensure that a genuine review takes place. Alternatively, a list of the criteria against which the schedule is to be measured may be helpful. While the particular questions or the criteria will be determined by the goals and expectations articulated in the planning processes, here are some suggestions:

- The hours the attorney agreed to work compared to the number of hours actually worked.

- A review of the work done by the attorney, including whether the work was completed on time and was satisfactory.

- The attorney's communication with and responsiveness to clients.

- The attorney's communication with supervisors and colleagues.

- Whether the attorney needs any additional technology or clerical help to be more effective.

- If any emergencies came up since the last review, whether the response of the firm and the attorney was appropriate.

- Whether any change needs to be made in the attorney's schedule or work assignments to achieve the desired balance.

- Whether the attorney has been able to engage in any continuing education, firm administrative work, or business development activities.

- Whether both sides are satisfied with the arrangement.

As a result of the review, it may be necessary to renegotiate the balanced hours arrangement between the firm and the attorney and amend the balanced hours agreement in writing.

■ Additional Considerations

A balanced hours policy does not stand alone but must coordinate with the firm's other policies and fit into the firm's culture. Here are a few things to consider.

Client Relationships

Given that a key reason for implementing a balanced hours program is to maintain client relationships, it makes sense to address client-related issues at the outset. An essential issue to address is whether clients will be told when an attorney moves from standard hours to balanced hours and, if so, how and by whom.

"No part-time program can work," Arnold and Porter's Managing Partner Jim Sandman has said, "unless clients are involved from the start." He has had discussions with clients who work with attorneys who want to reduce their hours. Once the clients understand that reducing hours will enable the attorney to continue to work with the firm and serve the client, they usually have no objection to the schedule change. Research by PAR's Corporate Counsel Project[6] confirms this experience. Typical responses by in-house counsel include:

- The client is served by a team of law firm attorneys, so one is always available and it doesn't matter to them who it is;

- Full-time attorneys are rarely at their desks all the time working on only one client's matter, so little difference is noted between the availability of full-time and part-time attorneys; and

- Experiences with part-time attorneys have shown them to be more concerned about responsiveness and deadlines, and no problems related to reduced schedules have been noted.

The firm may decide that whether to tell a particular client about an attorney's schedule depends on the particular client. In that case, receptionists and secretaries may have to be instructed to say that a reduced hours attorney "isn't at his desk right now" and to take a message, rather than saying "he isn't in yet" or "he has gone home for the

---

[6] In connection with PAR's second study about work/life balance in corporate law departments, corporate counsel were asked about their experiences working with attorneys in law firms who were part-time and their willingness to work with part-time attorneys. The overwhelming majority of respondents reported no difficulty or reluctance to work with part-time outside attorneys. PAR's report is available on its web site, www.pardc.org.

day," which sounds unprofessional. The firm may want to establish a system for referring calls to other attorneys.

A related issue is responsiveness; if the firm has a policy of responding to client communications within a certain timeframe, the firm's expectations with respect to how balanced hours attorneys will respond to clients may need to be articulated. The policy may require, for example, all attorneys who are out of the office, regardless of the reason, to check voice mail and/or e-mail every few hours and could state that the policy applies to balanced hours attorneys as well as standard hours attorneys.

Workload Management

Workload management, not just for balanced hours attorneys but for all attorneys, is intimately intertwined with schedule issues. How work is assigned, how the firm ensures that all attorneys are busy but not swamped, and how skill development is assured are all issues that can be addressed in a workload management policy. If the firm already has a workload management policy, it will need to be reviewed to ensure it is coordinated with the balanced hours policy.

In reviewing or creating a workload management policy, it is important to ensure that it addresses balanced hours attorneys expressly. An essential element is that a balanced hours attorney's workload be cut proportionally to his or her hours. Expecting a balanced hours attorney to get as much work done as a standard hours attorney is unreasonable and undermines the program. Workloads can be cut by reducing the number of clients the attorney works for or the number of matters he or she handles.

So, how does the excess work get done? The first and most obvious answer is to look at the workloads of the other attorneys in the firm or department to see if any are underutilized. This is not, however, an invitation to pile work on already busy standard hours attorneys. Such a move will quickly breed resentment and undermine a good balanced hours program. Another answer is to look at anticipated work needs and hire a part-time or full-time attorney if justified, or cross-train an attorney from another department.

A third approach, which may be optimal for senior associates and partners, is to redesign the work so that the balanced hours attorney has the same amount of work but is working smarter by performing the higher level work while supervising paralegals or associates to accomplish the more junior level work. Effective use of technology should also be part of this approach.

Technology and Technology Support

Many firms today give their attorneys technology allowances or provide certain technology to them. The firm's existing policies or practices with respect to technology should be reviewed to ensure they will sufficiently meet the needs of balanced hours attorneys if they are expected to be able to respond to clients outside of the office.

Laptops, BlackBerry® handhelds (or personal digital assistants with mobile e-mail), cell phones, extra phone lines, fax machines, remote access to the firm's computer system, and technical support are a few of the options that allow attorneys to stay connected regardless of location or time of day. Of course, technology also plays a pivotal role in productivity for standard hours and balanced hours attorneys.

PAR heard, however, that technology has created many frustrations for attorneys and can be a time trap. In one particularly illustrative story recounted in the PAR report,[7] an attorney told of working at home to complete a project with a short deadline only to have her attempts to send her work to her office take more than four times as long as doing the work had taken. Part of the problem was not having the best tools for the job — the attorney's firm wouldn't provide her with a fax to use in her home office and she couldn't afford to buy one at the time — and part of the problem was not having a support person she could call after hours to help her fix the problem that was preventing her laptop from logging on to the firm's computer to transfer her document.

Technology is expensive, but the upfront investment is repaid many times over in billable hours, satisfied clients, and happy attorneys. A $200 fax machine will pay for itself quickly if it enables an attorney to bill even one additional hour from home. When viewed this way, it is not hard to see that all attorneys, regardless of their work schedules, benefit from having access to the technology that best supports their work style. For example, an attorney who is frequently out of the office may need the ability to retrieve e-mail remotely, and an attorney who is not a quick typist may need a fax machine to send handwritten pages to a secretary. Some firms have opted, therefore, to give attorneys "technology allowances" rather than providing the technological devices themselves. Other firms, concerned about interoperability and performance standards, have provided attorneys with a limited choice of technological devices.

Either way, the job is only half done unless good technology support is provided. Depending on the size of the firm, in-house information technology (IT) staff may be able to be on call or it may be best for an outside vendor to be contracted to be available to resolve technology problems. In creating tech support plans, due consideration should be given to

---

[7] Joan Williams and Cynthia Thomas Calvert, "Balanced Hours: Effective Part-Time Policies for Washington Law Firms," Final Report, Second Edition (August 2001), at 39.

issues such as when and where tech support is most likely to be needed and whether training will be needed in addition to troubleshooting problems.

Additional Policies

Other policies that already exist at the firm may be impacted by the balanced hours program as well. Examples of policies the firm may want to examine are criteria for partnership, eligibility for bonuses and perks, assignment of administrative duties, use of support staff, security measures for confidential client documents that attorneys work on at home, and mentoring.

Chapter Summary

- The implementation team should decide at the outset what the process for drafting a policy will be; it may include appointment of a drafting subcommittee and review of the draft policy by key players in the firm.

- Balanced hours policies should be proportional in pay, benefits, bonuses, billable hour requirements, assignments, and advancement to prevent stigmatization.

- Balanced hours policies have to be flexible in order to work. The policies need to be available to all attorneys, not just caregivers, and they should be flexible enough to allow schedules that are individually tailored to the needs of specific attorneys. In addition, the policies have to be flexible in duration, allowing attorneys to work reduced schedules for as long as necessary and to move between reduced schedules and standard schedules without repercussion.

- Key components of a balanced hours policy that should be defined include eligibility for balanced hours, the process for requesting balanced hours, work expected and compensation offered, expectations regarding nonbillable work, the effect of a balanced hours schedule on advancement, the compensation policy for extra hours, and periodic review of the schedule.

- Other firm policies should be created or reviewed to address related issues such as client relationships, workload management, and technology.

Chapter 7

Implementing the Policy

Policies don't implement themselves. If a firm's commitment to a policy begins and ends with drafting it, the policy will wither on a shelf or, worse, create false expectations that damage management's credibility and erode associates' morale. True commitment exists — and success occurs — when a policy is not only drafted but also implemented in a way that firmly weaves the policy into the fabric of law firm life.

The key objectives in implementation are buy-in and follow-through. "Buy-in" means that all attorneys in the firm need to understand the business reasons behind the decision to institute a balanced hours program and the benefits the firm expects to gain from the program. It also means that the attorneys realize that the firm is committed to making the balanced hours program a success and that their support of the program is required. "Follow-through" means that the firm will consistently and repeatedly take steps that affirm the program, and will make achievement of the program's goals a priority in the firm's long-range plan.

Implementation can take many forms depending on the individual characteristics of a firm but always requires these elements:

- Leadership;
- Communication;
- Training; and
- Assessment.

■ Leadership

Leadership from the top is crucial. The firm's managing partners have a vision of the firm's future and can see how a balanced hours program is necessary to make that vision a reality. The task for these leaders is to extend that vision to others in the firm, to help others understand the important role a balanced hours program can play in the firm's goals and the important role each attorney can play in the program's success.

While leadership includes publicly stating support for the new program and its goals, leadership takes more than that. The leaders need to make the new program part of the firm's culture. In hallway conversations and lunchtime chats, they can talk about the new policy. In discussions of proposals for future firm business or activities, they can raise the issue of how the proposal relates to the firm's new policy. They can keep their doors open to those who have concerns about the new policy and allay those concerns. They can praise supportive actions and discourage actions that undermine the program.

One Managing Partner's Commitment

At Arnold & Porter, LLP, in Washington, D.C., it is hard to doubt the commitment of the firm to its part-time program. Managing Partner Jim Sandman understands first-hand the needs of attorneys to take care of responsibilities in their personal lives; when his son was born, he took a six-month sabbatical to take care of him and he has lived with the pull of parental responsibilities that occur without regard for business schedules. Jim is very vocal about the firm's part-time program, talking about it in bar association programs and to local news reporters. He consciously communicates his approval of the program, celebrating within the firm successes of part-time attorneys and visibly modeling behavior that prizes quality of work over hours of face time.

Leadership Action Points

- Drop by the offices of part-time attorneys and ask how their work is going.

- In a group gathering at the firm, praise the results a part-time attorney has obtained for a client or congratulate a part-time associate who has made partner.

- Make firm leaders aware that their own work schedules send messages about the relationship between hours and success at the firm and encourage leaders to work reasonable hours where possible.

- Ask part-time attorneys to work on matters for important firm clients.

- Speak at conferences and bar programs about the firm's part-time program.

- Appoint part-time attorneys to firm committees.

- Use contacts to get speaking engagements or article placements for part-time attorneys.

- Talk to partners who are not committed to the policy and explain that the future success of the firm requires their commitment.

- When the firm's attrition costs are reduced, when the firm has a great recruiting season, or when the firm lands a big client who cares about retention and diversity issues, point out the contribution the new policy made.

- When talking to the firm's clients, discuss the new policy and how it benefits the clients through more stable relationships, and assure the clients their needs will always be met.

- When the firm wins quality-of-life awards or other public recognition for its balanced hours program, issue a press release and send a note to clients.

- Make supervisors' evaluations, compensation, and promotions dependent, in part, on how effectively they implement the policy.

■ Communication

Communication is the centerpiece of an effective implementation program. A consistent message, repeated often and in a variety of ways, is the objective.

The Message

The message to be communicated is fairly simple: the firm has decided to institute a balanced hours program for sound business purposes, including improving retention and bolstering client relationships, and everyone is expected to work to make the new policy succeed. That message by itself, however, is unlikely to have any effect on the firm.

John Kotter of the Harvard Business School advises that the message must create a sense of urgency in the listeners in order to gain their cooperation.[1] Complacency, he says, kills initiatives that involve change, and a primary source of complacency is lack of a visible problem.[2] Therefore, a frank discussion of firm problems that a balanced hours program can be expected to address is a vital part of the message. If the firm's attorneys hear that the firm's finances are threatened because it has lost a major client, or the firm will not be paying large bonuses because attrition costs for the past year exceeded two million dollars, or the firm has been unable to attract the high-caliber attorneys it needs for a new practice area that is important to the firm's future success, they are going to be more receptive to the proposed solution.

Getting the Message Out

The method of communicating the message will necessarily have to be tailored to the particular culture at the firm but will likely include a mix of written communication (e.g., firm newsletters or memos), group communication (e.g., large or small meetings to explain the policy and the reasons for its adoption), and individual communication (e.g., one-on-one conversations between the members of the policy task force and individual attorneys).

Written communication. There is an advertising maxim that people need to see information three times before it registers. Effectively delivering a message about a new policy thus requires several communications. A memo from the firm's managing partners is essential; this memo should explain the substance of the policy, the business case for adopting the policy, and the implementation process. A sample memo is provided in the appendix. In addition, articles in the firm's newsletter or on the firm's intranet and an-

---

[1] John Kotter, *Leading Change* (Harvard Business School Press, 1996), at 36.
[2] Id. at 37-40, 45-46.

nouncements in firm or practice group meetings will spread the word. Each type of communication may be different, containing a higher or lower level of detail, but each will reinforce the notion that the policy is here to stay and everyone must abide by it.

> Deloitte Touche Tohmatsu has a link to its part-time policy on the first page of its intranet, where it can be seen every time its employees turn on their computers.

Group communication. Group meetings can be an effective way to educate people in the firm about the business necessities that drive a balanced hours program and about the specifics of the new policy itself. Group meetings are also an excellent vehicle for creating the group dynamics necessary to cause meaningful change at a firm.

Attendance is always an issue when planning group meetings. Requiring attendance may help; these meetings are, after all, about the future of the firm. It is easier for attorneys to attend if meetings are kept short and offered in multiple sessions at varying times during the day. Providing food, of course, is a time-honored method for drawing a crowd. These tactics not only help ensure participation but also send a strong signal about the importance of the new policy.

Who should run the meetings? It is important to have at least one or two key players at each meeting as well as a member of the implementation team who can lead the discussion. He or she can create for the attendees a sense of urgency regarding implementation of the program by explaining the business case and providing hard numbers to show the impact schedule-related problems have on the firm and its clients. The implementation team member can also strive to create a comfortable, collaborative atmosphere that encourages questions and the exchange of information. Firms that have decided to appoint a balanced hours coordinator (see Chapter 8) can let the coordinator explain the specifics of the policy and how it will be implemented.

Effective group meetings leave plenty of time for discussion at the end. A question and answer session allows the issues that are most important to the attendees to be addressed. The questions may well reveal skepticism and resistance to something new, but questioning, analyzing, and arguing are the ways lawyers work. Members of the change committee may want to close the meeting by encouraging attendees to meet with them individually if they have questions or concerns they wish to discuss further.

Sample Agenda for Group Meetings

I. Introduction by Key Player
    A. Purpose of meeting
    B. Importance to the firm of pursuing a path that will decrease attrition and increase attorney and client satisfaction

II. Introduction by Implementation Team Member
    A. Why is the firm pursuing this issue?
        1. Hard numbers regarding cost of unwanted attrition
        2. Composite stories about attorneys who left the firm and why
        3. Reaction of clients to attrition
        4. Benefits the firm expects to gain from new policy
    B. How was the policy created? Participants and the planning process
    C. Expectations of the firm regarding everyone's commitment to the policy

III. Discussion by Balanced Hours Coordinator
    A. Terms of new policy
    B. Plans to implement new policy

IV. Discussion by Committee Member Regarding Accountability
    A. Firm will ensure success of the policy, no one is allowed to undermine it
    B. All will be accountable through their performance evaluations, compensation, and promotion criteria

V. Discussion by Committee Member Responding to Potential Obstacles (Overhead, Floodgates, Professional Commitment of Balanced Hours Attorneys)

VI. Question and Answer Session

> **How to Encourage Discussion**
>
> - Give the questioner full attention, making good eye contact and being careful not to send nonverbal discouraging signals, such as crossed arms.
>
> - Begin answers to questions with remarks indicating appreciation of the question, such as "I'm glad you asked that," "That is a great question," "That raises a difficult issue that the committee had to discuss for a long time," and "That's very perceptive and important."
>
> - Answer directly and succinctly and then give a more elaborate answer.
>
> - Follow responses to questions by asking if anyone else in the room has something to add or has had a different experience.

Individual communication. Although harder to plan and more time intensive, individual communication plays a vital complementary role in developing necessary buy-in. It allows the implementation team to address concerns that an attorney might not voice in a large group, and it provides the perfect avenue to respond to the objections of individual attorneys who are resistant to change. Dropping by an attorney's office and taking an attorney to lunch are effective methods of promoting individual communication.

Manage the Nonverbal Message

A consistent message is crucial: The firm must make sure that its nonverbal messages match its verbal messages. Just as the words of a person who says "yes" while simultaneously shaking his or her head from side to side in a "no" motion cannot be trusted, attorneys will not trust words of support for the balanced hours program if the firm is sending nonverbal signals of nonsupport at the same time. Conspicuous silence from key players in the firm is a strong nonverbal message. So, too, are decisions relating to assignments, bonuses, and advancement after the balanced hours program is put into practice. The attorneys will see who gets the good work, what types of work or work styles are rewarded, and what actions smooth the path to partnership or firm management. If rewards are given only to those who work the most hours, the firm's words of support for the balanced hours program are irrelevant. The louder message getting through is that the firm isn't truly backing the new program and that the status quo is expected to remain the same.

Sustaining the Message

Communicating the program and the firm's commitment to it is not a one-time or even a several-time deal. To make the policy part of the fabric of the firm, leaders, other key players, and implementation team members must raise the issue every chance they get in casual conversations and meetings. Memos, group e-mail, or voice mail messages, and notices posted on the firm's internal computer sign-on screen can be issued and updated regularly. These messages can provide implementation updates and highlight successes, such as new clients that hired the firm as a result of the new policy, and provide current data related to how the balanced hours program is improving the bottom line. It would impress even the skeptics to see quarterly figures showing that applications for attorney positions are up, attrition is down, and costs have been cut.

> At Prudential Insurance Company, Peter Sayre, head of the tax department, waited patiently for a year after he instituted a new flexible work arrangement program. Then he held a town meeting where he publicized that those on flexible work arrangements had fared slightly better than those working a traditional schedule in their annual reviews. The usage rate of flexible work arrangements shot up.

■ Training

When firms introduce new ideas and ways of doing business to their attorneys, training is usually provided. A new computer system, revised billing methods, more stringent client service standards, and the like usually come with a few hours of mandatory instruction. A new balanced hours program requires a similar investment of time and energy to get off to a good start.

Two types of training are essential to make the program work: basic training to ensure that attorneys understand what the balanced hours program entails, why it is necessary, and how to make it succeed for the firm; and awareness training to overcome unexamined assumptions that can undermine a well-intentioned policy.

The content of basic training will vary depending on the audience. While there are some things everyone needs to know, some things will be specific to those who want to reduce their hours, those who supervise them, and those who work with them. A good argument can be made for exposing everyone to the same training — attorneys who have reduced their hours would benefit from understanding the perspective and goals of their

> At the outset, it may be useful for the implementation team to articulate the reasons for training. This will help tailor the training to the specific objectives of the firm and help everyone involved to understand the importance of training. Reasons may include the need to:
>
> - Ensure understanding of the parameters of the balanced hours program.
> - Foster communication among attorneys about expectations.
> - Increase professional effectiveness of attorneys who have reduced their hours — as well as the effectiveness of their supervisors and colleagues.
> - Develop awareness of spontaneous and unexamined assumptions and feelings that can undermine the success of the program.
> - Emphasize the importance to the firm of the success of the balanced hours program.
> - Promote accountability for making the program work.
> - Prevent resentment and backlash.
>
> The firm's objectives — however they are defined — should serve as a blueprint for program and training development and as a yardstick for measuring achievement.

supervisors and vice versa — but the size and resources of the firm may make this impractical. The following lists suggest focal points of basic training for the key constituencies involved.

Basic Training for Everyone

- The business case for implementing a balanced hours program (feedback from clients regarding attrition, statistics demonstrating attrition and its costs, survey data and research reports showing potential improvement in recruiting).
- The terms of the balanced hours program (who can work balanced hours, how balanced hour schedules will be monitored and evaluated, compensation, benefits, advancement).
- Communication and expectations of clients (how good client service will be ensured, whether and how clients will be told of reduced hours arrangements).
- Accountability for success of program (everyone is accountable and how support of balanced hours schedules will factor into evaluations, bonuses, and compensation, as discussed in the next chapter).

- Measurement of success (short-term and long-term goals, periodic evaluations of effectiveness of program, feedback and troubleshooting, as discussed in the next section).

Basic Training for Attorneys Who Want Balanced Hours

- Development of a balanced hours proposal (the pros and cons of different types of balanced hours schedules, consideration of business needs, how current caseload will be altered, how emergencies will be handled, approval process).

- Communication between balanced hours attorneys and others in the firm (availability when not in the office, responsiveness to clients, communication with colleagues and subordinates regarding status of work, accountability to supervising attorneys).

- Professional effectiveness (appropriate use of technology, time management, realistic setting of deadlines, supervision of subordinates when not in the office).

- Handling schedule creep (introduction of objective measures designed to identify schedule creep and avenues for redress).

- Open door policy (avenues for discussing problems).

- Evaluation of the success of individual schedules (frequency of review and criteria).

- Professional development (remaining active in bar and firm activities, making time for business development and CLE).

Basic Training for Supervisors

- Determination of appropriateness of balanced hours proposals (judging proposals solely based on business needs, criteria established by firm for acceptance of proposals).

- Management of workload (reducing the caseload of balanced hours attorneys, redistribution of work, ensuring balanced hours attorneys continue to have challenging assignments).

- Assistance for attorneys on balanced schedules (ensuring availability of proper technology and clerical support, helping to communicate with clients, encouraging balanced hours attorneys to remain active in bar, firm, and CLE activities, guarding against schedule creep).

- Supervision of balanced hours attorneys (judging quality and not face time, setting reasonable expectations, appropriate communication when attorney is out of the office).

- Communication of support for balanced schedules (explaining how negative talk undermines the business goals of the program, addressing legitimate equity concerns, maintaining relationships with balanced hours attorneys).

- Open door policy (avenues for discussing problems).

- Evaluation of balanced schedules (frequency of review, criteria for judging success, remedies for problem areas).

Basic Training for Colleagues

- Explanation of the business case for effective balanced hours programs, stressing the firm's commitment to the program for business reasons.

- Availability of the program to anyone who can make the business case for a specific proposal — not just for mothers of young children.

- Statement that balanced hours attorneys are making financial trade-offs in exchange for flexibility and are being offered only proportional pay and advancement — that people who work longer hours will still be rewarded for their extra work.

- Discussion of the practices necessary to work successfully with balanced hours attorneys (communicating about status of cases, maintaining relationships).

- Distribution of workload (management's plan to ensure that no one is overburdened).

- Open door policy (avenues for discussing problems).

Awareness Training

Attorneys on nonstandard schedules often face assumptions that are barely conscious, yet deeply influential. Unseen and unaddressed, these assumptions feed negative attitudes that are communicated subtly in every interaction between balanced hours and standard hours attorneys. Subtle biases prevent the firm from truly embracing the concept of balanced hours as a business necessity, and they send messages of disapproval to attorneys who choose to reduce their hours. Much of the disadvantageous treatment of part- and full-time attorneys involves unexamined bias that can be addressed only by bringing it to a conscious level and discussing it.[3]

The best way to address assumptions is through training conducted by an experienced professional trainer. Why? Addressing assumptions can stir up deep feelings and strong opinions, which may even be influenced by religious and political beliefs. If not handled delicately and in a constructive manner, articulating the assumptions can be divisive to a firm's workforce or even give rise to discrimination claims. When handled properly, the discussion of assumptions and their effects can strengthen relationships and create a healthier work environment, as well as ease the path toward a beneficial balanced hours program. Some firms already have diversity training and could incorporate the balanced hours awareness training into the existing program. Others need to initiate a new program, which should be provided for all attorneys and staff.

Research in recent years has documented the kinds of spontaneous and unexamined assumptions that can derail a balanced hours program even when top firm management is committed to its success. In one such study, Susan Fiske and Peter Glick report that women who are perceived as "businesswomen" are rated as high in competence, alongside "businessmen" and "millionaires."[4] In sharp contrast, women who are perceived as caregivers are rated as low in competence, alongside (to quote the researchers' stigmatized words) "the elderly," "blind," "retarded," and "disabled." This research provides important background for understanding a now famous comment made by a female lawyer: "When I returned from maternity leave, I was given the work of a paralegal. I wanted to say: 'Look, I had a baby, not a lobotomy.'"[5] The Fiske and Glick studies suggest that by taking maternity leave this lawyer had, according to one commonly held perception, fallen out of the high-competence "businesswoman" category into a low-competence "caregiver" category. This perception is not a matter of ill will; it is a spontaneous assumption, and it will persist as long as it remains unexamined.

Awareness training sessions can help to bring this kind of assumption to the surface. For example, awareness training sessions run by Deloitte were designed to tease out the ways we all tend to make different assumptions about men and women. In one scenario in a Deloitte training session, a man and a woman were both late to a meeting. Referring to

---

[3] Linda Hamilton Krieger, "The Content of Our Categories: A Cognitive Bias Approach to Discrimination and Equal Employment Opportunity," 47 *Stanford Law Review* 1161, 1193-94 (1995).

[4] Fiske, S.T., Cuddy, A.J.C., Glick, P., and Xu, S., "A Model of (Often Mixed) Stereotype Content: Competence and Warmth Respectively Follow from Perceived Status and Competition," *Journal of Personality and Social Psychology*, 82, 878 (2002).

[5] Williams, J. and Segal, N., "Beyond the Maternal Wall: Relief for Family Caregivers Who Are Discriminated Against on the Job," *Harvard Women's Law Journal*, 26 (2003).

the woman, someone says, "Oh, she must have had daycare problems." To the man, the comment is: "What's the matter, ole' buddy? Are you getting too old to handle the late nights?" In actuality, the man had been up late due to his son's fever; the woman's delay was due to a train derailment. The training program featured small group discussion of the scenario, the assumptions, and the actual facts. As a result, the unexamined became examined, and destructive assumptions were weakened or even eradicated.

A similar format could be useful in teasing out assumptions regarding lawyers and balanced hours. In addition to assumptions discussed in psychological studies such as competence assumptions, the awareness training could cover the growing business school literature that documents the conceptual confusion between "face time" and commitment. For example, training could examine the assumption that someone who works fewer hours is less committed to the job.

Examples of Unexamined Biases

Prescriptive bias: A male partner informs a woman associate that his wife has her hands full even though she's at home full-time and he doesn't see how one can be a good lawyer and a good mother at the same time. He is enforcing a traditionalist notion of how "good" mothers should behave.

Descriptive bias: "When a man says he cannot make an 8 o'clock meeting because he has to take his children to school, somehow the meeting is magically rescheduled, and everyone thinks he's a great guy. But when a woman says she can't make it for the same reason, somehow the meeting is not rescheduled, and it's further evidence she's not committed to her career," notes Dotty Lynch, Senior Political Editor for CBS News. In other words, observers may attribute the same behavior to different reasons depending on what they believe to be purely objective descriptions of the behavior of men and women.

Here's another example: If a person working reduced hours can't get something done on a given day, the reduced hours schedule is generally blamed, whereas if persons who are working full-time can't get everything done, they are considered overburdened.

Methods for Conducting Training

Law firms use a variety of methods to train their associates: programs featuring outside professional trainers; seminars taught by in-house attorneys; small brown bag lunch discussion groups; monthly lectures; roundtable discussions; practice group meetings; videoconferenced and satellite live presentations followed by discussions; videotaped presentations; self-study modules; CD-based learning; Internet-based learning; learn-by-doing workshops; and one-on-one training. Often a single firm will use four or five of these methods, fitting the method to the topic. A combination approach would work well for training related to balanced hours. For example, basic training might consist of seminars and small group discussions. Follow-up training in one-on-one sessions could be set up to address individual issues, and CD-based tutorials could help attorneys create their balanced hours proposals. Training to overcome assumptions may be best handled through presentations from outside trainers or in roundtable and small group discussions.

Deloitte's Training Program

In the early 1990s, Deloitte began the process that led to its innovative flexible work arrangement program with series of small group discussions and workshops. Management personnel, divided into groups of 24, attended workshops that addressed issues of gender in the workplace. Outside facilitators were brought in, and videos, discussions, and case studies were used. The group broke up into smaller groups to discuss the case studies and then report solutions back to the larger group. One-on-one conversations about personal experiences supplemented the learning in the workshops. As a result, hidden assumptions were exposed and examined, and a genuine attitude shift took place. (McCracken, Douglas M., "Winning the Talent War for Women: Sometimes It Takes a Revolution," *Harvard Business Review*, Nov/Dec, 2000.)

Additional training followed. In the mid-1990s, Deloitte developed written materials to educate its employees about flexible work arrangements. These included an informational brochure, an implementation guide, and an information package. In 1998, Deloitte held additional workshops, designed to teach management skills related to the flexible schedules. The same year, Deloitte developed CD- and intranet-based materials aimed at individuals who wanted to work flexible schedules and began to develop a mentoring program.

Training, of course, is not a one-shot deal. A good reason to vary the methods used for training is the need to sustain interest for subsequent trainings. Training will also have to be provided for new arrivals, and using methods such as videotape followed by discussion may be a cost-effective option.

> ## Leveraging Experience at Ernst & Young
>
> Flexible work arrangements have been in place at Ernst & Young for several years, yet the firm believes that the process of cultural change is an ongoing process. It makes use of a variety of methods. In one recent event, Ernst leveraged its experience by asking employees who were successfully using flexible schedules to advise other employees in an area that was just starting to revamp its work arrangements.
>
> It held a Flexible Work Arrangement (FWA) forum in Boston for everyone in the New England area who wanted to attend. Partners on FWAs elsewhere in the firm were flown in because the area didn't have a lot of FWA role models. First, they met with the partners, principals, and directors to answer all their questions about how to make flexible schedules work. Then, later in the day, the same FWA partners held a forum for everyone in the area who was interested in changing their schedules. The FWA partners provided a frank discussion of their real-world experiences, pitfalls, and successes — an invaluable training experience.

Ensuring Attendance

Getting lawyers to attend a training session can be extremely difficult. It will likely take an edict issued by the firm's managing partner to get attorneys to attend in significant numbers. When Deloitte held two-day workshops for its employees in 1992 and 1993 about gender-based assumptions that prevented women from staying with the firm, it required its management personnel to attend.[6] Its CEO at the time, Mike Cook, personally monitored attendance. One partner reportedly remarked, "Resistance was futile."[7] The results are impressive: More than 5,000 Deloitte professionals, including the board of directors, the management committee, and managing partners of all Deloitte's offices in the United States, attended the workshops.[8]

---

[6] McCracken, Douglas M., "Winning the Talent War for Women: Sometimes It Takes a Revolution," *Harvard Business Review* (Nov/Dec 2000).
[7] Id.
[8] Id.

■ Assessment

Periodic assessment of the progress of implementation ensures that the program's objectives are being met. It provides an assessment of the effort to date, offers direction for the implementation team's further work, and highlights obstacles that need to be addressed. Assessment has a more strategic purpose as well. As is discussed in greater detail in the next chapter, when an assessment reveals that progress is being made, there is evidence that the balanced hours program can provide tangible benefits to the firm. This, in turn, builds credibility for the implementation team, creates momentum for continued implementation, and quiets critics of the program. Assessment is therefore crucial to the implementation process.

What, when, and how to assess? As the implementation team draws up its plan of action, assessment points can be included. Items to assess could include: effectiveness of group meetings in building a consensus; usefulness of awareness training in starting a firm-wide dialogue on assumptions, gender, and work styles; changes in the number of attorneys reducing their hours; response of applicants to the firm's new program; and costs saved due to increased retention of talented attorneys. Some of these items, such as the effectiveness of meetings and trainings, will be assessed when completed; others may be assessed at regular intervals such as quarterly or semi-annually. While some assessments can be made using demographic statistics and accounting information, the more subjective assessments can be made only by taking the pulse of the firm through surveys and informal conversations. Once measured, the results need to be communicated to firm managers, and if any follow-up actions are indicated, they need to occur.

 **Chapter Summary**

- The key objectives of implementation are buy-in and follow-through.

- Implementation requires leadership, communication, training, and assessment.

- Firm leaders need to communicate clearly and frequently how the balanced hours program relates to their long-term vision for the firm. They also need to communicate their support for the program and their expectation that everyone in the firm will similarly support the program.

- The message communicated to the firm must create a sense of urgency by tying the goals of the program to solving real problems for the firm. Written, group, and individual communication methods should all be used.

- Training should include basic training for everyone on issues such as the business case for implementing the program, what the program is, and accountability for success of the program. Individual attorneys who want to reduce their hours, supervisors, and colleagues of those who have reduced their hours may need additional training targeted specifically to their circumstances.

- Training should also include overcoming assumptions about attorneys who reduce their hours to eliminate attitudes that can undermine the success of the program. Training of this sort is best carried out by a professional trainer.

- A variety of training methods, such as small group discussions and live videoconferenced presentations, can be used. Training is not a one-shot deal, and different methods may be more appropriate for refresher training or for the training of new attorneys.

- Periodic assessment is necessary to measure progress and to build momentum.

Chapter 8

Making the Program Work on a Firm Level

Any time a new program is implemented, the challenge is to make the program a lasting success. This means removing obstacles, providing incentives, and sustaining momentum. Strategies aimed at making the new balanced hours program successful are just as important as the new part-time policy itself. This chapter presents some ideas for success.

■ Appointing a Balanced Hours Coordinator

In a recent study of part-time work at law firms, 61% of all respondents said that no one at their firm had worked with them to develop their reduced hours arrangements.[1] Nearly 80% reported that no one at their firms met with them on a regular basis to discuss how their balanced hours arrangement was working.[2] PAR's study reached similar conclusions and additionally found evidence that, at some firms, the attorneys who have been placed in charge of supervising part-time programs are not perceived as being supportive of attorneys with reduced hours and have actually driven attorneys from the firm.

Appointing a balanced hours coordinator — a partner who has worked reduced hours or who understands first-hand the need to juggle competing roles in life — can be the essential element that allows a firm to reap the full rewards of a balanced hours program. The coordinator provides the counseling and guidance balanced hours attorneys and their supervisors need, and also monitors hours and assignments to keep the program on track. He or she can be responsible for training attorneys at the initiation of the program and for follow-up or new attorney training. The coordinator also serves as a visible symbol of the firm's commitment to the program and, ideally, as a role model.

Dickstein, Shapiro, Morin & Oshinsky LLP, in Washington, D.C., has experienced the benefits of having a balanced hours coordinator. Called the "Alternative Schedule Ad-

---

[1] Women's Bar Association of Massachusetts, "More than Part Time: The Effect of Reduced-Hours Arrangements on the Retention, Recruitment, and Success of Women Attorneys in Law Firms" (2000) (available at http://womenlaw.standford.edu/mass.rpt.html).

[2] Id.

> **Functions of a Balanced Hours Coordinator:**
>
> - Collect and provide information about balanced hours at the firm.
> - Help attorneys and firm plan balanced hours proposals.
> - Monitor schedule creep and assignments.
> - Address excessive hours with supervising attorneys.
> - Advocate and support balanced hours attorneys.
> - Provide training about the program initially and thereafter for new attorneys.

visor," she is a partner who is an advocate and a resource for attorneys exploring or working reduced schedules. The partner, Gabrielle Roth, herself works reduced hours and made partner while doing so. Ms. Roth not only helps lawyers develop their proposals for reduced hours, she also monitors their assignments. Dickstein Shapiro keeps track of the disparity between the schedule an attorney has agreed to work and the actual hours worked to prevent schedule creep — a strategy also employed by other law firms with a demonstrated commitment to balanced hours, notably Morrison & Foerster in San Francisco and Palmer & Dodge in Boston. While Ms. Roth's job includes meeting with supervisors of balanced hours attorneys if schedule creep needs to be addressed, the situation has rarely arisen.

■ Backlash Prevention

The media have reported on a backlash — feelings of frustration experienced by full-time employees who must work longer hours to do work that used to be done by employees who have reduced their hours. Feelings of frustration may be compounded by the fact that often the employees who have reduced their hours are parents and the full-time employees are not; personal attitudes about being child-free may increase friction and tension for some individuals, and perceptions may arise that parents are receiving more favorable treatment. If these feelings of frustration and resentment are not managed, they will be a powerful force that dooms a balanced hours program to failure, and the results will include damaged morale, reduced productivity, and increased attrition.

There are three key methods for preventing backlash, and they should be used together for maximum effectiveness. The first is workload management. As discussed in

Chapter 6, it is critical that the hours and workloads of full-time attorneys not be increased as a result of implementation of a balanced hours program. Similarly, it is important that the balanced hours program address who will be available for last-minute assignments and how such assignments will be made; if every time an emergency arises at 5:00 pm on a Friday afternoon, a standard hours attorney is expected to work all weekend while a balanced hours attorney is expected to go home, resentment will flourish. (Addressing such emergency situations is discussed in Chapter 10.)

The second key to preventing backlash is to make balanced hours available to everyone. If balanced hours arrangements are treated as individual accommodations or "secret side deals" for superstars or mothers, the people who are not offered the opportunity will feel they are not as valued, or they may feel that the choices they have made about their personal lives are not supported by their employer. They may even feel resentful enough to quit, or to make claims of discrimination. If, on the other hand, all employees have the option of reducing their hours and their pay, the employees who work full-time do so by choice. Having consciously made a decision to work for more money or faster advancement, they cannot blame their employer for their schedule.

The third method of preventing backlash is to manage employee relationships. One way of doing this is to use awareness training (Chapter 7) to eradicate assumptions about commitment and professionalism on the part of balanced hours attorneys and to improve communication between standard hours and balanced hours attorneys. A firm may have to have several refresher seminars or more advanced training — or offer sessions with a coach. Another way of managing relationships is to provide an outlet for the expression of negative feelings; for example, the firm might name an ombudsperson or designate a partner with an open door policy. Just as a firm would address the recalcitrance of an attorney who did not follow the firm's policies with respect to client service or business generation, it needs to address the recalcitrance of an attorney who refuses to follow the balanced hours policy.

■ Balanced Hours Information Database

Lack of information and an absence of role models have hampered many part-time programs. How can individuals who want to cut back their hours learn what makes a reduced schedule successful, the pitfalls to watch for, the various forms that reduced schedules can take, the best way to communicate with clients, and the like?

Recognizing the difficulties presented by this traditional information vacuum, Deloitte and Ernst & Young created databases filled with information about flexible work arrangements. Through their desktop computers, for example, all employees of Ernst & Young have instant access to such information as the types of flexible work arrangements available; the schedules and experiences of employees on flexible work arrangements who have agreed to be resources; explanations of how to negotiate a flexible work arrangement; and descriptions of success factors.

> ### A Database Example
>
> When Deborah Holmes arrived at Ernst & Young, she found what most companies have today: flexible work arrangements that were rarely used. She decided to end the secrecy and let the light shine in. She e-mailed every person in the company, asking them to share publicly their experiences if they were on a flexible work arrangement. Five hundred and fifty agreed to do so, and Holmes and her team created a database that profiled each one: what each thought had worked well, how they made things work, and what their challenges were. The database also contained worksheets and other resources to help employees work out the kinds of flexible work arrangements that would be effective for them.
>
> This database was put on the desktop of every Ernst & Young computer, with a gateway consisting of a message from the Chairman expressing his commitment to work/life issues. The usage rates of flexible schedules jumped. Holmes credited the communication: "I believe in the power of the grassroots. If you put tools in the hands of 27,000 people, 27,000 people will make it happen."

■ Hold Partners Accountable

Employers who get serious about balanced hours as a program vital to their bottom-line success have incorporated their managers' success in implementing the program into their salary calculations:

- At Ernst & Young, partners' compensation is set pursuant to four factors, one of which concerns effective management of human capital within the firm.

- At Pillsbury Winthrop, LLP, practice group managers are held accountable financially for attrition. "A well-run group will watch the make-up of their group, and if there is a problem they will look into it and report to the managing board," said Mary Cranston, Chair and CEO. If attrition is higher than expected, managers go in and see "whether a practice group head is weeding people out" or is losing top performers. "We are not passive about these things. If there is a lack of mentoring or a problem with a partner, we expect group heads to come to us with solutions." If problems persist, partners will feel it in their wallets. Cranston concludes: "Very bad attrition because of a failure to manage or a failure to make the workplace friendly for everyone is a particular factor in compensation."

Linking partner compensation to implementation of a balanced hours program will ensure the program's success. It is a logical linkage. Firms implement balanced hours programs largely for financial reasons, and financial rewards for promoting the firms' financial goals make sense. On the flip side, the failure to support the program causes firms to lose money, and recognition of the losses in setting the compensation of the responsible partners is not only rational but a step toward remediation.

There is no clearer way to communicate that firm management is serious about making a balanced hours program work. Management would not sit idly by if partners openly disregarded other crucial firm policies. Making support of the balanced hours program a factor in the compensation equation places the program on equal footing with other business-related policies and goals.

Performance Evaluations

"When a lifestyle that requires one to push all non-work obligations aside on a regular basis is viewed as a symbol of commitment and a sign of merit, it is difficult for associates to make different choices even if they are not interested in partnership in the immediate future."[3] Attorney performance evaluations are a vital management tool. Traditionally, whether an attorney has met the target for billable hours has been a major criterion in evaluations, but evaluating and rewarding long hours over good quality work sends the wrong message. An effective way to make balanced hours a successful part of the firm's culture is to de-emphasize the ability to work long hours and to emphasize excellent work, creative thinking, and high-quality client relationships when making annual evaluations and at partnership decision time.

---

[3] Boston Bar Association Task Force on Work-Life Balance, "Facing The Grail: Confronting the Cost of Work-Family Imbalance," June 1999, at 21.

■ Eliminate Myths about Commitment

In addition to judgments made in evaluations, a firm needs to separate the ability to work a certain schedule from the perception of being a "valued team player." Often supervisors and attorneys working standard hours are unaware that they equate face time with whether someone is "committed to the law" or "committed to the firm." Professor Lotte Bailyn of the Massachusetts Institute of Technology points out that this is typical; many employers confuse the issue of *who has talent* with the issue of who puts in more "face time."[4]

Of course, having talent is not the same as being a "hard charger"; attorneys with mature judgment, strong skills, extensive experience, and sterling interpersonal relationship skills play significant roles in the long-term vitality of the law firm regardless of the number of hours they work. It is important, therefore, that supervisors make sure they send verbal and nonverbal messages that talent is appreciated irrespective of schedule in their daily interactions with attorneys. It is equally important that firms ensure that *everyone* in the firm understands that attorneys can remain committed professionals even though they have decided to reduce their hours.

Without a doubt, this is easier said than done. When Deloitte faced this challenge, it responded by creating mandatory workshops for all accountants on "Men and Women as Colleagues." All participants were asked to define the characteristics of a committed professional. The men tended to equate commitment with long hours and to assume that people working in flexible work arrangements were less committed. The women did not. They tended to assume, given the difficulties in working reduced hours, that those in flexible work arrangements were more committed: otherwise, they would simply have quit. "On most days I am taking care of children or commuting or working from the moment I get up until I fall in bed at night," said one lawyer quoted in a Boston Bar study. "No one would choose this if they weren't very committed."[5]

Workshops such as those instituted by Deloitte may help law firms to overcome serious but often unrecognized impediments to a successful balanced hours program. Diversity trainers can facilitate such workshops, and it may be possible to incorporate a discussion of work/life balance, commitment, and performance in the diversity programs some firms already offer. Other ways to disarm unexamined assumptions include articles in firm newsletters by empirical psychologists or sociologists, and discussions between mentors and protégés or in practice groups and partners' meetings. The separation of com-

---

[4] Lotte Bailyn, *Breaking the Mold: Women, Men, and Time in the New Corporate World* (Free Press 1993) at 44-46.

[5] Facing The Grail, supra note 3, at 25.

mitment and schedule could be strengthened by public recognition and advancement of attorneys who perform well on balanced hours schedules.

■ Celebrate Successes

Change takes time, and maintaining momentum can be difficult. Recognizing interim benefits gained and losses avoided helps sustain the focus on the importance to the firm of having balanced hours. It also diminishes resistance to change caused by feelings of "there's no way things will change around here" or "not in my lifetime."

Said another way, celebrating "short-term wins" will help the firm see that its efforts are paying off and serve as evidence that ultimate success is achievable.[6] In addition to reinforcing the firm's vision and goals, such recognition can reduce any negativity generated by the unbelievers. It also provides feedback to the key players and rewards the individuals who have worked hard to implement the program.

The sort of short-term wins that deserve recognition are those that are visible, unambiguous, and clearly related to the balanced hours program.[7] Hyping every little accomplishment or claiming victory based on an event that would have happened regardless of the balanced hours program will smell fishy — or worse — to the firm's attorneys. The short-term wins can come about as a result of goal setting and planning, periodic assessment, or serendipity, but, however they come about, firms shouldn't miss an opportunity to crow.

■ Coaching

Individual coaching is becoming popular today among corporate executives, managers of all types, and lawyers. Coaches help their clients identify objectives, develop strategies for accomplishing the objectives, and put the strategy into action. A key role played by coaches is that of neutral, trusted advisor who can help to work around obstacles in order to maintain forward progress. Lawyers are using coaches with increasing frequency to help them develop business, improve relationships and personal effectiveness, and balance their professional and personal lives.

Group or individual coaching can be very beneficial in the implementation of a balanced hours program, particularly as a follow-up or add-on to training sessions. A coach can help individual attorneys who want to balance their hours to work effectively and manage their professional stature within the firm. Coaches can counsel supervising attorneys

---

[6] Kotter, John P., *Leading Change* (Harvard Business School Press, 1996), at 117-124.
[7] Id. at 121-22.

Some of the successes a firm might recognize include:

- Completion of the infrastructure necessary to support the balanced hours program (policy, technology, training).
- Reduced attrition by firm or practice group, or specific key departures averted.
- Significant recruiting costs saved.
- Strategic or high-profile attorneys hired because of the program.
- Positive comments from clients.
- Advancement to partnership of balanced hours attorneys.
- Good publicity in the local or national press.
- Successes achieved for clients by balanced hours attorneys.

How can successes be celebrated?

- Notices on the firm's intranet or internal computer sign-on screen.
- Articles in the newsletter.
- Firm or departmental lunches, happy hours, or parties.
- Memo to partners with their draw checks stating increase in profitability over prior years due to reduced attrition.
- Press releases.
- Mementos or prizes given to attorneys who have contributed to successful implementation of the program.
- Bonuses paid to the balanced hours coordinator or to practice group heads based on retention.

about relationships with balanced hours attorneys; coaching focused on personnel issues related to balanced hours within a practice group could be a very effective way to overcome resistance on the part of particular attorneys. An important role for coaches is simply to keep up the momentum toward full implementation of a successful balanced hours program. Working with the managing partner or the group in charge of implementing the program, a coach can point out unexamined assumptions or interpersonal dynamics that may otherwise undercut well-intentioned initiatives.

> ## Coaching Is Good for Business
>
> Washington, D.C.-area coach Ellen Ostrow, Ph.D., is working with an increasing number of attorneys who seek her help with developing a client base — an undertaking they have little time for as they juggle the competing demands of work and personal lives. Balanced hours attorneys in particular benefit from business development coaching, she says, because meeting the needs of their clients often leaves little time for traditional rainmaking activities. A focused marketing strategy, some brushed-up skills, and a few tips about making contacts in creative ways can put them on the path to having their own book of business.

■ Fill the Firm with Supporters

When hiring lawyers and staff, a firm looks for individuals who will fit in well with the firm's "culture," or the norms of behavior and the shared values of the firm.[8]

Once a firm has decided that a balanced hours program is or should become part of its culture, it is logical to require that applicants' attitudes toward balanced hours be considered in determining how well they will fit. Similarly, attitudes toward balanced hours can be considered in determining whether to retain an individual; firms tell attorneys and staff that their talents would be put to better use elsewhere for a variety of reasons, and incompatibility with the firm's objectives and vision is a valid reason to suggest alternate employment. Ensuring that the firm is peopled with individuals who support balanced hours is a sure way to make the program succeed.

---

[8] Kotter, John, *Leading Change,* supra note 6, at 148-49.

Chapter Summary

- A balanced hours coordinator can keep the program on track, troubleshooting and guiding as necessary. Establishing this position shows the firm's commitment to the program as well.

- Active management of the firm's or practice group's workload will help prevent schedule creep. The number of clients or matters can be reduced for balanced hours attorneys or work can be redesigned.

- Backlash can be prevented by not shifting work from balanced hours attorneys to standard hours attorneys, making balanced hours available to everyone, and managing employee relationships.

- Providing a database of information about the balanced hours program, including personal experiences of attorneys who have changed their hours, makes the program more usable.

- Accountability for implementation of the balanced hours program is crucial to obtaining results. Firms can make implementation a factor in the review and/or compensation process. Given that a balanced hours program and a firm's financial performance are linked, accountability in financial terms makes sense.

- Evaluation criteria should be examined to ensure consistency with the objectives of the balanced hours program.

- Ending confusion between face time and professionalism is vital if the balanced hours program is going to achieve its intended results for the firm. A culture that prizes the ability to sit behind a desk for long hours over high-quality work is unlikely to have a non-stigmatized program.

- As the firm begins to reap the benefits of its new program, recognize the successes publicly. Celebrating small wins sustains the momentum toward successful implementation.

→ Coaching for individuals or small groups can smooth implementation. Coaches can address pockets of resistance to the new program and increase effectiveness of balanced hours attorneys and their supervisors.

→ Criteria for hiring and retention of attorneys and staff should also be consistent with the objectives of the balanced hours program. Support for an important firm objective is a legitimate consideration in determining whether an individual fits into the firm's culture.

Chapter 9

Making the Policy Work on an Individual Level

In a traditional part-time program, individual attorneys typically bear sole responsibility for making their schedules work. Even if schedule creep occurs or a lack of technology hampers their productivity, anything less than stellar success may be taken as a reflection on the program as a whole. In a balanced hours program, individual attorneys have a proactive role to play in making their schedules work, but a firm can help by creating an appropriate schedule and requiring planning (as discussed in Chapter 6), providing support from mentors and other balanced hours attorneys, offering feedback, maximizing effectiveness, communicating with supervisors and clients, and ensuring professional development.

■ Creating an Appropriate Schedule

Creating the appropriate type of schedule is a basic ingredient for success. If an attorney's needs outside the office would best be addressed with fewer hours per day, setting up a schedule to work fewer days per week is not going to work. Issues for the attorneys to consider include:

- What schedule does the attorney need to balance work and an outside life? For attorneys who want to travel, teach, do intensive volunteer work, or further their education, working a full-time schedule for eight or nine months of the year and not working at all the remaining months may make sense. For a nursing mother, working a five- or six-hour day five days a week may be a good routine. For an attorney with elder care or childcare responsibilities, working fewer days per week may be best.

- What type of schedule is necessary to meet work obligations? A litigation practice that frequently requires attendance at day-long depositions or court hearings may work better with a schedule of several long days per week rather than five shorter days, for example. Attorneys may find it helpful to talk to others who have worked balanced hours, whether in the firm or elsewhere, to find out what types of schedules have allowed them to be successful at work.

- To what extent is the attorney willing to be contacted by colleagues or clients when not in the office? Some attorneys have no trouble blending work and personal roles, while others find it necessary to draw a bright line between the two. PAR's research showed that an ability to blend roles is an ingredient in successful reduced hours work but also indicated that open communication of expectations or desires about how and why an attorney's roles would overlap is even more crucial.
- If the attorney is reducing hours because of caregiving responsibilities, how will those responsibilities be handled if the attorney has to work at a time when he or she was scheduled to be off?
- How does the attorney plan to stay integrated into firm life, including social events? This is too important an issue to leave to chance. Attorneys planning to reduce their hours should plan time to have lunch with colleagues and attend firm events.
- If the schedule an attorney wants is not available, what other schedules might work and what other options might the attorney consider?

Balanced hours schedules will likely need to change over time as the professional work and outside lives of lawyers change. This process of creating an appropriate schedule may need to take place several times to adjust for changes. The "Balanced Hours Schedule Checklist for Attorneys" provided as Appendix 4 may be a useful tool for attorneys engaged in this process.

■ Support Groups and Mentors

Mary (not her real name) told PAR investigators that she was thinking of leaving the firm where she was working part-time. She was getting good work, her clients supported her schedule, and she rarely had to work more hours than budgeted. But she no longer viewed herself as a rising star at the firm, and she had a nagging feeling that others in the firm shared that view. After nearly an hour of conversation, she found the root of her disquiet. All her life she had been an over-achiever: top schools, straight A's, distinction for excellence in extracurricular activities, and growing recognition in her community as the go-to attorney for tough commercial litigation. Stepping back her schedule meant giving up the fast track and renouncing her bid to be superhuman. It did not matter that the activities she was planning to undertake in her personal life would be extremely important and fulfilling; at a deep emotional level, she felt that choosing to be a mere mortal at her firm meant she was less than adequate. Uncomfortable with her feelings of inadequacy, which were compounded by the messages of decreased worth received from her firm, she was considering leaving her firm and perhaps the law.

John (a pseudonymous composite) was also troubled during his interview with PAR. He was not as bothered by feelings of inadequacy as Mary, but he felt he was struggling uphill to make his balanced hours schedule work. He was the first man at his firm to reduce his hours, and in fact he was currently the only part-time attorney at the firm because the two women who had been working part-time had both left. He felt he was having to spend time reassuring others at the firm that he would be able to hold up his end of the work, and that was time he could have put to better use working for his clients. He also felt unsure about his future at the firm, primarily because he couldn't envision a path to partnership for an attorney working reduced hours.

As discussed in Chapter 2, in most firms few role models and little support exist for attorneys who are trying to balance their schedules. Attorneys seeking to reduce their hours have to invent or reinvent the wheel and often feel isolated as they move forward. Many attorneys interviewed during the PAR study expressed strong, sometimes negative, feelings that they could not discuss with other attorneys for fear of increasing the stigma of working part-time.

Firms have a role to play in preventing these negative feelings from undermining balanced hours attorneys' quests for success. The biggest role is working to eliminate stigma, as has been discussed frequently in this book. In addition, firms can provide support and role models.

Support can be informal, in the form of casual social gatherings or brown bag lunch discussions. A number of firms already have "women's groups" or "mothers' groups" for female attorneys, and it would not be difficult to expand these to include men and the topic of balanced hours. Support can also be more formal, such as in providing professional coaching. Coaching can be one-on-one or in small groups. One coach in the Washington, D.C. area, Dr. Ellen Ostrow, provides coaching to male and female attorneys on the topic of balanced hours and has found that attorneys' busy schedules make group coaching via telephone conference a popular alternative.[1]

Mentoring is another area in which firms are already active. Studies by The NALP Foundation and others have shown that mentoring is a highly desirable offering, affecting both recruiting and retention.[2] In existing mentoring programs, new associates are typically paired with more experienced associates, and senior associates with partners, to enhance job satisfaction, professional development, and business development. While it would not be difficult to extend existing programs to include balanced hours mentoring, firms may find themselves with a shortage of mentors who have experience working

---

[1] LawyersLife Coach Web site, http:www.lawyerslifecoach.com (last viewed on 7/9/04).
[2] The NALP Foundation for Law Career Research & Education, *Keeping the Keepers: Strategies for Associate Retention in Times of Attrition*, at 40-41 (1998); Abbott, Ida, *The Lawyer's Guide to Mentoring* (NALP, 2000).

part-time successfully. Mentors can be recruited from other offices of the firm. (Recall the method used by Ernst & Young mentioned in Chapter 7: Faced with a dearth of alternative work role models, the Boston office flew in alternative work partners to advise its employees and partners.) Other firms or bar associations, particularly women's bar associations, may also be a source of mentors, but issues of confidentiality will have to be addressed.

■ Providing Feedback

Recent studies have also shown that, in addition to mentoring, young associates want frequent and specific feedback.[3] Attorneys working reduced hours will appreciate being told how their schedule is working and asked for their perception of its effectiveness, particularly if the person providing the feedback is not one who would ordinarily be involved in a formal review process. Frequent and casual feedback as part of an ongoing effort to foster open communication provides encouragement and allows problems to be nipped in the bud. Feedback should supplement, not supplant, the formal periodic reviews discussed in Chapter 6.

Feedback Examples

- "We certainly appreciated the hard work you put in on the Jones matter. Your effort certainly paid off!"

- "I saw you had to stay late on Thursday night to draft the response to the TRO application — thanks. It looks like we're going to have some more short deadlines coming up. Would it help to get Mary Ann more involved in this case?"

- "You responded well to Ms. Client's questions, but next time please call her back sooner. As you know, our department's goal is to return all calls within four hours and we agreed it is reasonable for you to check your voice mail twice a day on your days off. If you aren't going to be able to check your voice mail when you are out of the office, please have your secretary check your messages and forward the ones from clients to me."

---

[3] *Keeping the Keepers*, supra, at 39-40; Pierce, Linda Green, "Gen X Change the Rules," available at http://www.nwlegalsearch.com/articles/generation_x.html.

■ Maximizing Effectiveness

When attorneys reduce the number of hours they spend in the office, it is important that they be able to put all their office time to the best possible use. Making technology available can be helpful, as discussed in Chapter 6, but only to the extent that attorneys are encouraged to use it and trained to use it properly. Many attorneys still shy away from learning new software applications or don't understand how they can automate many of their tasks. Brown bag lunches or breakfast sessions to talk about innovative uses of existing technology could significantly improve productivity.

Appropriate delegation can boost effectiveness tremendously but is an area, again, in which attorneys may need encouragement and/or training. All too often, an attitude of "It's easier to do it myself" prevails, and this is a losing strategy in the long run. Attorneys may need to be coached on how to give assignments to secretaries, paralegals, and junior attorneys, how to track and follow up on the assignments, and how to give feedback after the conclusion of an assignment. Good personnel management skills are not innate, and attorneys may need to be instructed about how to develop relationships with those to whom they delegate, how to avoid micromanagement, and how to treat assignments as an opportunity to help others develop professionally. Supervisors may want to be on the lookout for situations in which these types of delegation skills can be fostered.

Effectiveness can also be enhanced by simple time management techniques. Some attorneys may benefit from a refresher seminar on how to recognize which tasks are important and urgent and which tasks are not,[4] and on basic skills such as how to handle e-mail and phone calls so as to minimize the disruption to their day. Others may benefit from learning how personal digital assistants and personal information management software can help them keep track of work and upcoming deadlines. Making this kind of information available will pay off in increased productivity.

■ Communicating with Supervisors and Clients

A balanced hours schedule is headed south if a supervisor does not know whether an attorney is going to be able to meet an important deadline — or, worse, if the supervisor does not find out until after a deadline has passed that the attorney was not able to meet it. Similarly, if clients are left wondering when they can next talk to their lawyer, or whether anyone is actually working on their matters, relationships can quickly become strained. The only way to prevent these stresses and strains is regular, frequent communication.

---

[4] Covey, Stephen R., *7 Habits of Highly Effective People* (Simon & Schuster, 1990).

Communication about status of work is so important that firms are strongly encouraged to manage the communication proactively. Communication is just as important for standard hours attorneys, of course, and whatever system the firm sets up will likely benefit the firm as a whole. Supervisors and attorneys may choose one or several methods to exchange information — phone calls, e-mails, group communication software, memos, or meetings — each of which can be scheduled daily, weekly, or as frequently as the type of work requires. The objective should be to find a quick and easy method that gets the information to the people who need it. Here are some examples:

- The attorneys who work on a particular large matter can get together for coffee on Monday and Thursday mornings to discuss the status of each attorney's projects.

- A firm can use the messaging and calendaring software on its computer system to keep track of work. Each attorney can list the tasks he or she is working on, including the percentage of work completed, the due date, and comments. The task lists of each attorney can be made available to other attorneys with whom the attorney works. Software can be set to regularly remind supervisors to check the task lists of the attorneys they are supervising.

- A supervisor and attorney can agree that at the end of every day the attorney will send a short e-mail to his or her supervisor stating what has been done and what still needs to be done on particular projects. These communications will have the added benefits of helping attorneys to better manage their workloads and supervisors to look for opportunities to coach for better productivity.

Communication with clients similarly is so important that firm-wide systems are advisable. It is fashionable today for firms to have a rule that all client calls are returned within 24 hours, and some go further with a four-hour rule. Of course, such rules should also apply to balanced hours attorneys. Firms with these types of rules often establish a back-up method for handling client calls; when an attorney is unreachable, for example, his or her secretary may be instructed to refer phone messages to another attorney to handle.

In addition to returning calls, attorneys should be encouraged to initiate calls to clients to check in with them. Such calls build client trust and loyalty, and give clients the opportunity to mention additional legal needs that may have arisen. In the case of balanced hours attorneys, these types of calls will reassure clients regarding the continued accessibility of the attorney. Of course, attorneys have to be sensitive to each client's preferences for timing and manner of communication; some busy in-house counsel may be annoyed by unnecessary interruptions of their work.

■ Ensuring Professional and Business Development

Attorneys who have reduced their hours often admit that the first things that get cut from their schedules are professional and business development activities.[5] These activities are so important, however, to both the attorney and the firm that a firm would do well to make encouragement of professional and business development activities a formal goal. Encouragement can occur informally during chats between mentors and protégés, or be more institutionalized by holding attorneys accountable for completing certain development-related activities as a condition for receiving a good performance review or a bonus.

Suggestions for Encouraging Professional and Business Development

- Hold seminars or write newsletters for clients and potential clients and ensure that balanced hours attorneys are involved.

- Ask partners to share speaking or writing opportunities with junior attorneys, with special care to include those working balanced hours.

- Advertise educational or relationship-building opportunities on the firm's intranet.

- Sponsor bar activities at the firm and encourage the firm's attorneys to attend.

- Provide coaching sessions for individuals or small groups to help attorneys create time and identify non-traditional opportunities for marketing.

- Provide educational experiences in-house at convenient times or in several short sessions, to make it easier for balanced hours attorneys to attend.

---

[5] Joan Williams and Cynthia Thomas Calvert, Project for Attorney Retention, "Balanced Hours: Effective Part-Time Policies for Washington Law Firms," final report, second edition (August 2001), at 25.

Chapter Summary

- An appropriate schedule is fundamental. If the schedule does not address the attorney's needs outside the office, it cannot be a success.

- Firms can create or expand existing support groups to help balanced hours attorneys cope with the questions and emotions that often accompany a reduction in hours. Mentoring and coaching can also be provided.

- Frequent, ongoing feedback about how the new schedule is working can help make the schedule successful. Younger attorneys are particularly interested in receiving feedback.

- Technology, delegation, and time management techniques can make an attorney more productive. Providing instruction and encouragement in these areas will help attorneys and their firms realize an increase in effectiveness.

- Many problems and misperceptions relating to balanced hours schedules can be avoided with good and frequent communication. All attorneys should communicate with their supervisors and clients, and firms have a role to play in establishing systems to make sure the communication takes place.

- Balanced hours attorneys often have trouble finding time for professional and business development activities. Firms can encourage them to participate in such activities, and can offer opportunities to make it easier for them to do so.

Chapter 10

Common Myths and Frequently Asked Questions

"Balanced hours may work for a firm that does real estate work, or trusts and estates. But there is no way it can work at our firm because we do a lot of litigation."

Successful balanced hours attorneys exist in all practice areas. PAR interviewed commercial litigators, mergers and acquisitions attorneys, and white-collar defense attorneys, to name a few practice areas that are generally considered to require too many hours for an attorney to work a reduced schedule. These attorneys had cut their hours and nevertheless were regarded as highly competent and effective in their chosen fields. Ultimately, PAR found successful balanced hours attorneys in every practice area that had been asserted as unsuitable for part-time. The pattern that emerged was that a balanced hours schedule was successful where a supervisor was receptive to it and was unsuccessful where it was not supported. In other words, it is not the practice area but the supervisor's attitude that is the key.

Commercial litigation can be used as an example to show that the assumption that litigation always requires a standard schedule can be wrong. Commercial litigation frequently involves complex cases with many issues, witnesses, documents, and proceedings, and teams of attorneys typically work on one matter. The team approach lends itself to balanced hours work, not because work can be shifted from balanced hours to standard hours attorneys but because the team's workload can be managed to make the most of each attorney's time. Additional attorneys can be brought on to the team, paralegals and technology can be utilized, and availability can be considered along with skills when work is assigned. Moreover, emergency deadlines are typically the exception rather than the rule in large commercial cases, and balanced hours attorneys can plan their schedules so they work more hours as a deadline draws near and fewer hours after it has passed. Here is how one balanced hours attorney managed her litigation schedule:

> "For several years after my children were born, I worked part-time and spent most of my time on insurance coverage litigation. The cases were very large and involved many attorneys. I was a senior associate and

later a junior partner during this time, and I was in charge of one portion of a major case and assisted on other portions. For the portion that I managed, I set deadlines that were consistent with my schedule. I scheduled depositions and expert witness conferences on days when I could be in the office all day. On shorter days, I researched, reviewed documents, prepared for depositions, and wrote motions briefs. We worked under a case management order, so I knew well in advance what my deadlines were. I tried to pace the work so I didn't end up with a lot of last-minute work when the deadline got near, but I also knew that I had to make sure I had someone at home who could watch my children around deadline time in case I had to stay late.

"When I had out of town depositions or hearings, I tried to schedule as many depositions and meetings as I could for each trip to minimize the number of trips I had to make, and I worked long hours while traveling to take advantage of the fact that I didn't have to be home at a certain time. During trials, I pretended I was out of town and turned childcare over to my spouse and babysitter. When I returned from travel or ended a trial, I took several days off to be with my children and catch up on things that had to be done at home."

A second response to this question involves taking a creative approach to scheduling. A balanced hours schedule does not have to mean fewer hours per day or fewer days per week but can be molded to fit the needs of the particular area of practice. Just like the litigation attorney who was quoted above, many M & A attorneys find they have to work long hours or even through the night on occasion as important deadlines loom. If they want to reduce their hours, they may find they are more successful if they plan a reduced number of hours over the course of a year, working a greater or lesser number of hours during specific points in the year in response to their workloads. The key to this approach is making sure that they actually do take time off when they can.

A third response is that successful balanced hours attorneys become very organized. We all know that many work crunches stem from poor planning, where a deadline has been on the books for weeks but no one starts to focus on it until several days beforehand. An attorney committed to controlling his or her schedule will develop hitherto undeveloped skills at careful planning to prevent avoidable crises.

"Philosophically, balanced hours are fine. But our firm is focused on client service, and the clients are not going to put up with part-time attorneys."

Have you asked your clients about part-time attorneys? When you do, you may well find that your assumptions are dead wrong. Without a doubt, stopping turnover is critical, as one senior in-house counsel said: "Stability is extremely important. Outside lawyers who have an institutional memory are incredibly valuable to us."[1] As Jim Sandman stated in his remarks to the ABA (see sidebar on following page), clients recognize that a key to keeping the attorneys with whom they have developed a history and a relationship is helping them to create work/life balance.

Moreover, the concept of balanced hours may not be as foreign to clients as it is to firms — and may even be viewed as a plus. Many large companies are recognized annually as good places to work, often because they have viable alternative work schedules.[2] Others are recognized publicly for the work they do to promote minorities and women, including addressing schedule issues.[3] Working with balanced hours attorneys is consistent with these clients' philosophies. On an individual level, many of the clients are seeking balance as well, and some are working alternative schedules to do so.[4] Even those who are not themselves concerned with balance may well expect a law firm to take such issues seriously because they understand the business reasons for doing so: According to work/life consultants, corporations have taken issues of balance far more seriously, and made far greater strides, than have law firms. Many corporate clients work in an environment where work/life initiatives have been in place for years.

The best way to respond to concerns that clients will not accept part-time attorneys is by seeking information from clients themselves. In PAR's Corporate Counsel Project, one of the issues studied was how corporate counsel, as clients, react to outside counsel who work reduced hours.[5] As discussed in the Project's final report, an overwhelming majority

---

[1] Catalyst, *Women in Law: Making the Case* (Catalyst 2001) at 24.
[2] E.g., "100 Best Companies to Work For," *Fortune Magazine*; "The 100 Best Companies for Working Mothers," *Working Mother Magazine*.
[3] E.g., Minority Corporate Counsel Association (annual award given to "Employers of Choice" that demonstrate a commitment to hiring, retaining, and promoting minority attorneys).
[4] "Better on Balance? The Corporate Counsel Work/Life Report," Project for Attorney Retention, final report (December 2003), available at www.pardc.org. Another study also found high support among clients for part-time work by law firm attorneys: Only 17% of the lawyers surveyed in the Catalyst study said that clients are uncomfortable working with lawyers with reduced schedules. Catalyst, *Women in Law*, supra note 1, at 42.
[5] "Better on Balance?" supra note 4, available at www.pardc.org.

Client Reactions to Balanced Hours

Whenever I have heard this issue – the issue of the alleged incompatibility of part-time work with good client service – discussed among lawyers, whether at managing partner roundtables or at bar conferences or elsewhere, I am always struck by the fact that there is not a single client in the room. Not one.

I believe that the assumptions so many lawyers make about the negative impact of reduced hours on client service are uninformed and simply wrong. I would suggest that when this issue, or any client service issue, is discussed, clients be included in the dialogue, and I am glad to see the client community represented here at this summit.

My own conversations with our firm's clients are *uniformly* at odds with the common assumption about the incompatibility of reduced hours with good client service. Some of the most passionate advocates of our firm's part-time policy are *clients who are working with part-time lawyers*. Do you know why? There are two reasons.

The first is that these clients have an investment in the lawyer working a reduced schedule. That lawyer knows the client's business and knows the client's legal problems. The client has a self-interest in retaining that lawyer and often realizes that, if the lawyer were not working part-time, he or she would not be working full-time but instead would leave the firm to do something else. Smart clients know that reduced hours schedules are an important tool in retaining people of value to them, and they are happy to help make those schedules work.

The second reason why clients are supportive of part-time lawyers is that they do, in fact, get good service from those lawyers. Part-time lawyers, in my experience, are every bit as professional as full-time lawyers. They do not somehow lose their sense of responsibility or commitment to their clients because they are not working full-time. They communicate with their clients about their schedules and they work with their clients to be sure the clients' needs are met. They are flexible when the client's needs require it. I have never had one client complain about poor service from a part-time lawyer, and I have had a number volunteer their appreciation for our part-time lawyers.

In short, talk to clients about part-time arrangements. You will find that the assumptions about their dissatisfaction with those arrangements are dead wrong.

— James Sandman, Managing Partner, Arnold & Porter LLP (excerpt from remarks at "Summit on Keeping Her in Her Place: New Challenges to the Integration of Women in the Profession," Section of Litigation, American Bar Association; August 11, 2002).

of corporate counsel interviewed stated their support for part-time outside counsel. Comments similar to these were representative:

- "My outside counsel is not available to me all the time anyway because of travel, depositions, and commitments to other clients, and he works full-time. I don't notice a difference if someone works part-time."
- "A team of attorneys at the law firm works on our matters. If one isn't available, another one usually is."
- "I haven't had any problems. The part-time attorney was very conscientious about returning my calls and responding to my e-mails, and I never knew if she was in the office or out."[6]

Firms can ensure that excellent client service is provided by balanced hours attorneys — and standard hours attorneys — by actively managing workloads. A key point is that achieving balance often will involve not *slower turnaround* time but *fewer matters*: not skimping on service to existing clients but rather having balanced hours attorneys take on fewer cases or clients. Said one New York attorney:

> "Clients are only paying for the time they're getting. They are getting the same service. By getting me, they are not getting any different service than they got when I was full-time.... I think all of the women who want these concessions are professionals and are willing to be flexible — if something comes up and if someone is on a three-day work schedule and it is one of the days they are supposed to be off and a client says, 'I'm flying in from France, and this is the day I'm going to be there,' they are going to juggle their schedule and be there for the client..... I think clients are much more flexible than the lawyers. Clients are dealing with it in their own businesses and are finding ways to deal with flex-time and childcare. Law firms are not willing to do this yet."[7]

In some situations lightning speed turnaround is required; in others it is not. It is in the client's interests to be able to distinguish one situation from the other. This process will sometimes require initiating a conversation with a client about how best to handle

---

[6] These are composite comments and not actual quotes. Actual quotes can be found in the Project's final report.

[7] Cynthia Fuchs Epstein, Robert Saute, Bonnie Oglensky, and Martha Genver, "Glass Ceilings and Open Doors; Women's Advancement in the Legal Profession, A Report to the Committee on Women in the Profession," The Association of the City of the Bar of New York, 64 *Fordham Law Review* (1995), 15 291, 404.

workflow so as to minimize turnover on the client's account. To accomplish this, one law firm in Australia initiated a seminar about work/life issues and invited their clients. They found it highly successful at opening a dialogue between lawyers and clients about work/life issues.[8]

"Been there, done that." — "We tried part-time and it didn't work."

Advocating a balanced hours program is especially difficult in situations where part-time hasn't worked in the past. Perhaps the whole experience left a bad taste in everyone's mouth.

The first step is to analyze what went wrong. Sometimes the problem is that a part-time attorney was unreasonable, insisting on leaving every day like clockwork, or never working on the designated day off regardless of the circumstances. Some part-time attorneys are difficult — just as some full-time attorneys are. Sometimes the problem is that a part-time program wasn't well designed or implemented and consists simply of a series of ad hoc arrangements that benefits only a few attorneys — or that the program exists as nothing more than a piece of paper in a file and is a policy that attorneys were discouraged from using. But the failure of one part-time arrangement or program does not erase the business case for an effective and usable balanced hours program. Taking a candid look at the experiences of the past and how they can be used to build a stronger foundation for a balanced hours program can prevent similar failures in the future.

"We need go-getters — 'Part-time' signals 'part commitment.'"

Sometimes people say out loud that part-time means partial commitment; more often it's an unspoken message that nonetheless is sent — and received — loud and clear. Said one balanced hours lawyer: "On most days I am taking care of children or commuting or working from the moment I get up until I fall in bed at night. *No one* would choose this if they weren't very committed."[9]

The sense that balanced hours attorneys are not committed arises because of the common confusion between "face time" and "commitment."[10] Sometimes these two also are confused with talent. Think of the term "go getter": Does it mean someone who is talented or someone who is always there? The answer is that the two are often confused. If avail-

---

[8] Interview with Eileen Applebaum, Joan Williams, March 2001, Washington, D.C.
[9] "Facing the Grail: Confronting the Cost of Work-Family Imbalance," Boston Bar Association (1999) at 25.
[10] Lotte Bailyn, *Breaking the Mold: Women, Men, And Time in the New Corporate World* (Free Press 1993) at 44-46.

ability 24/7 is used as a proxy for talent and commitment, lawyers — to be successful — need not only talent and commitment but also a certain family structure. Either they can have a family where their partner provides virtually all of the family childcare, or they can decide that they feel comfortable leaving their children in paid care for ten, twelve, or even fourteen hours a day.

Defining "commitment" in this way systematically disadvantages women. Few families feel it is appropriate to leave children in paid care for virtually all of their waking hours. This leaves only the second option, which is open to many men but few women. A study by Catalyst found that nearly 28% of married men surveyed reported that they provided 100% of the family income. Only 5% of the married women did.[11]

Psychologists suggest some reasons for the common patterns of confusion. Studies have found that people who are coded as "businessmen" or "businesswomen" are rated as highly competent, but people coded as "caregivers" are rated as extremely low in competence. Given that lawyers typically reduce their hours for reasons relating to family caregiving, perceptions may change for lawyers who reduce their hours because — at a semiconscious level — they fall from the high-competence "businessperson" category into the low-competence "caregiver" category.[12]

A related impression is that part-timers cannot be counted on during crunch time. Sometimes this perception stems from the false impression that balanced hours attorneys will leave like clockwork regardless of whether or not there's a crunch deadline. If a balanced hours attorney actually does feel entitled to be unaffected by crunch deadlines, the attorney's attitude may reflect a lack of adequate training. As was discussed in Chapter 7, training is essential for the attorney who wants a balanced hours schedule. Every firm needs to help these attorneys think through crucial issues, such as how they are going to handle childcare during periodic crises when the need arises to increase their hours. In the case of an attorney with childcare concerns, clarifying up front that a balanced hours arrangement cannot work unless back-up childcare provisions are in place will avoid a lot of bumps in the road.

When a balanced hours attorney seems unwilling to accommodate crunch times, sometimes the problem really is the attorney. But often a larger dynamic is at work. Balanced hours attorneys may become rigid, for example, if they feel that they consistently accommodate crises only to find that they are treated as slackers when they try to take off "comp time" after the crises are over — or, worse yet, if they never even dare to take

---

[11] Catalyst, *Women in Law*, supra note 1, at 12.
[12] Fiske, S.T., Cuddy, A.J.C., Glick, P., and Xu, S., "A Model of (Often Mixed) Stereotype Content: Competence and Warmth Respectively Follow From Perceived Status and Competition," *J. Personality & Soc. Psychol.*, 82, 878 (2002).

"comp time" because they receive signals that taking comp time would be interpreted as a lack of commitment. In an environment where agreed upon balanced hours schedules are not being respected, a rigid insistence on being out the door at a predetermined time may seem the only way to protect oneself.

This situation can be avoided through proper training, as discussed in Chapter 7. If supervisors understand the need to respect balanced schedules and if coworkers clearly understand that balanced hours attorneys have traded money in return for time and that they can do so too, then a firm's culture will support the kind of reciprocity necessary for successful implementation of usable and effective balanced hours.

"It's not worth it to offer part-time because the part-timers end up quitting anyway."

If many part-timers quit, a firm should view the numbers as a warning of problems with the part-time program. Schedule creep is a likely culprit. If a balanced hours attorney finds himself or herself handling so many matters that crisis mode becomes a permanent condition, the balanced hours attorney may find that, in effect, he or she is expected to work a full-time schedule at part-time pay. Few people will work full-time at part-time pay forever, so one common response is to quit. This reflects not the inherent unworkability of part-time schedules but problems with implementation of a balanced hours program.

When levels of attrition among balanced hours attorneys are high, stigma may also have played a role. Even attorneys who do not experience schedule creep may leave if they find themselves with a steady diet of unchallenging or undesirable assignments. Attrition will naturally be higher among employees who feel they are "going nowhere."

A response sometimes heard from a frustrated part-time attorney is to "do what I can" and then leave, accepting the reality that finishing all the work assigned is impossible in the agreed upon schedule. Obviously, this response is less desirable than having an attorney confront the situation directly, but in some situations a balanced hours attorney may feel unable to bring up the problem, particularly if no formal mechanism exists for doing so. A firm that has implemented a balanced hours program — complete with careful planning to ensure that realistic expectations exist on both sides — is much less likely to encounter this kind of difficulty.

Another cycle is worth mentioning. Sometimes attorneys on balanced schedules feel that schedule creep reflects a failure by the firm to honor its commitment to provide and support balanced hours. Some part-time attorneys see coworkers' refusals to honor their schedules as a sign of disrespect.

Obviously, in a firm where balanced hours are implemented effectively, both the firm and reduced hours attorneys remain flexible. This works for a simple reason: Each side experiences reciprocity. Balanced hours attorneys know that if they work long hours to meet a deadline, they will be able to cut back once the crisis is over without being perceived as lacking in commitment. The trust and flexibility of the firm is met by trust and flexibility in return.

"If we let one go part-time, soon everyone will want to."

A widespread fear is that an effective balanced hours policy will open the floodgates, and all attorneys will want to reduce their hours. In fact, this has not happened at any firm. Firms that have worked hard on work/life issues, such as Arnold & Porter, Dickstein Shapiro Morin & Oshinsky LLP, Hogan & Hartson L.L.P., Palmer & Dodge LLP, Morrison & Forrester LLP, Davis Wright Tremaine LLP, and Perkins Coie LLP, find their usage rates top off at between 7% and 11%.[13] Moreover, relatively high usage rates are not the death knell for firms in any event; firms such as Palmer & Dodge and Harris, Wiltshire & Grannis[14] have remained highly profitable.

There are many reasons the floodgates do not open. First, some attorneys do not want or cannot afford to take a cut in pay. Second, some attorneys may want to reduce their hours for only a few months to attend to pressing personal issues and then return to standard hours. Third, some attorneys are content with the amount of time they have outside of the office. Fourth, some attorneys plan to have a phased career, where they work standard hours for a number of years to accumulate money or to develop to a certain level professionally and then make a career change. An effective balanced hours program is beneficial even for attorneys who choose to work standard hours. It allows them to choose the schedule they work, and the balanced hours option provides a safety valve that is there in the event it is needed.

"We can't afford balanced hours during a recession."

A balanced hours program may actually be a law firm's best tool to survive in a recession. A balanced hours program benefits a firm's bottom line and long-term viability, as discussed in Chapter 1. In addition, it is an inexpensive way for a firm to keep attorneys

---

[13] See Joan Williams and Cynthia Thomas Calvert, Project for Attorney Retention, "Balanced Hours: Effective Part-Time Policies for Washington Law Firms," final report, second edition (August 2001), at 48; *NALP Directory of Legal Employers* (2001).

[14] See Williams and Calvert, "Balanced Hours: Effective Part-Time Policies for Washington Law Firms," supra note 13, at fn 83.

happy and to have a flexible workforce that can shrink without painful layoffs if the level of work shrinks.

The assumption that work/life benefits will be cut during a recession reflects the view that flexible work arrangements are an expensive employee benefit — not an integral part of effective long-term management of human capital. A firm under the financial stress of a recession needs to do everything it can to run an effective and efficient business in the long run. For example, if a recession means that a firm's summer program is not quite as lavish as it was in the flush years, then it is all the more important to identify the "keepers" — and to keep them. If a recession means that a firm cannot offer bonuses quite as rich as in the flush years, it is all the more important to signal respect for lawyers' personal lives — and in fact to respect that many people have families, and other goals and dreams, as well as a strong work ethic and professional commitment.

Businesses don't ditch part-time programs during a recession. A survey of U.S. employers by Hewitt Associates found that nearly all forms of work/life programs experienced modest growth during the 2001-2002 recession. Said Carol Sladek, who worked on the survey: "The results don't surprise me, since most companies realize that offering work/life benefits is one of the best ways to boost morale during difficult times."

According to an interview on National Public Radio, Jim Sandman, Managing Partner of Arnold & Porter, agrees. Even in a recession, his firm does not cut flexible schedules, paid parental leave, or the firm's daycare center: "It would be penny-wise and pound-foolish to do away with benefits like that. The savings in the relative scheme of things would not be significant, and the impact on employee morale, on people's attitudes about what kind of place they are employed by, would be very adversely affected. It would be a stupid thing to do."[15]

Finally, having a workable balanced hours program in place gives firms an alternative to layoffs if personnel costs need to be cut. Attorneys will not be afraid to take a sabbatical or reduce their hours in response to economic pressures if they know they will not be hurt professionally by doing so. Conversely, few attorneys will dare work less than full-time in a law firm that has a stigmatized part-time program.

---

[15] James Sandman, interview on Minnesota Public Radio's Marketplace, September 2, 2002.

"Our firm has two tracks, an 1800 billable hour track and a 2100 billable hour track. Doesn't that achieve much of what a balanced hours program is supposed to achieve?"

Establishing two partnership tracks can have many of the same positive results as a balanced hours program, provided that a two-track program is implemented in a careful way to avoid creating a stigmatized "mommy track." Because two-track systems allow more time outside of the office and typically allow attorneys in the lower track to remain eligible for partnership, they can be helpful in recruiting and retaining talented attorneys. A balanced hours program is more effective at providing schedules that are tailored to individual needs, however. Even 1800 billable hours per year is more than some attorneys can work.

"Part-time causes problems for us because part-time attorneys can't be available to help with those late Friday crises, and that causes resentment from the full-time attorneys who have to stay."

There are two answers to this question. The first is that a firm should not assume that a balanced hours attorney cannot stay to help with an emergency. Often, particularly if the emergency involves a client or matter with which the balanced hours attorney has been working closely, he or she will be willing to stay. Even if this is not the case, a balanced hours attorney might be willing to stay in order to be involved with a high-profile or interesting assignment. Asking, rather than assuming, is best.

Second, when the firm implements a balanced hours program, it should address workload management issues. Every effort should be made to avoid late Friday crises: Work should not sit on partners' desks all week while a deadline approaches and be assigned only at the last minute, and clients should be asked what their true deadlines are. In addition, crisis work should be spread around to avoid resentment. The balanced hours policy should state how available balanced hours attorneys should be for emergencies, and the firm may want to consider instituting an "on-call" policy for all attorneys to provide advance notice that they are likely to have to work on any emergencies arising during a given weekend.

"We can't allow new associates who are just joining the firm to work part-time because a lot of learning goes on after hours when the partners are more available."

Allowing new attorneys to work balanced hours from the outset is a boon to recruiting, but so is informal contact with partners, which recruits realize can lead to important mentoring relationships and easier assimilation into the firm's culture. If a firm wants all new attorneys to work standard hours for a period of time to take advantage of relaxed evenings at the firm, the required period of standard hours should be as short as possible. Six months may be a reasonable amount of time to require.

Other alternatives should also be considered. For example, the firm might explain up front to new balanced hours attorneys that the firm wants them to spend some time at the firm in the evenings and that their schedules should be set up accordingly. An attorney may be scheduled to work late every Wednesday for a period of time, for example, and he or she could come in late on those Wednesdays as well. In addition, other opportunities for informal contact can be set up, such as breakfasts or lunches, or bar events.

"Surely balanced hours aren't the only answer to the retention problem!"

Schedule-related issues are one of the biggest factors driving attorneys from firms.[16] A balanced hours program recognizes this fact and squarely attempts to deal with it. Firms can, and should, look at other programs in addition to balanced hours they can offer to improve the job satisfaction and quality of life of attorneys. Some of these might include telecommuting, flexible hours, mentoring, and training. Very successful retention programs, such as those at Ernst & Young, Dickstein, Shapiro, and Deloitte, have used an approach that combines several initiatives. The centerpiece of the programs for each of these employers, however, was a program to allow employees to work fewer hours.

---

[16] See Williams and Calvert, "Balanced Hours: Effective Part-Time Policies for Washington Law Firms," supra note 13, at 8-10.

"What about staff? Do we have to let them work balanced hours, too?"

The answer is that it is a very good idea to extend balanced hours programs to legal staff. Recruiting and retaining good legal staff is critical to the long-term health of a law firm. Moreover, if lawyers are allowed balanced hours schedules without opening up the same option to support personnel, bad feelings often result.

At the law firm of Maslon Edelman Borman & Brand in Minneapolis, 13% of the support staff work alternative schedules. This includes eight legal secretaries, a librarian, someone in the business office, and three paralegals. The alternative arrangements include two secretaries who job share. Part-timers generally work three to four days a week. "We have no hard and fast policy," said Sandy Callen, the head of Human Resources. "Various employees have approached us about alternative work arrangements, and where we can we accommodate them." In fact, the firm has hired some support personnel on a four-day-a-week schedule. When secretaries work a four-day week, typically the remaining day is covered by a floater.

"It's a very tight labor market, even tighter for legal secretaries and paralegals. Law firms have had to implement some life balance type programs," said Callen. "We tend to be pretty open-minded when people need to come in late, leave early — we tend not to micromanage those types of things as long as they're able to get their work done and it works well with their supervisors. There have been occasions when we've had to say no, but we are more than happy to be as flexible as we can."

Firms that have allowed flexibility to support personnel have found a number of advantages. Maslon Edelman found that a key advantage of job sharing is that finding a replacement becomes the responsibility of the job-sharing employee rather than the supervisor. The firm also found that flexibility helps in recruiting: When the firm advertised a job-share for a human resources support position, they got a "deluge" of applications. "We had a hot ticket!" said Callen.[17] Other employers have found that having two part-timers improves coverage. For example, if one can come in early and leave early, while the other comes in late and leaves late, coverage is available for more hours than on a standard schedule. In addition, some employers have found that, in the event of a work crunch, it is much easier to bring in trusted permanent part-time employees rather than to rely on temps.[18]

---

[17] Joan Williams, *Unbending Gender: Why Family and Work Conflict and What to Do About It* (Oxford University Press 2000), at 90.

[18] Id. at 92-93.

Appendices

Appendix 1

Sample Memo to Firm Regarding New Policy

MEMORANDUM

To: Firmwide Distribution
From: Pat Jones, Managing Partner
Re: Balanced Hours Policy

I am pleased to announce that our firm's Management Committee has adopted a Balanced Hours Policy. The policy, a copy of which is attached to this memo, creates a reduced hours program for attorneys and staff.

In a nutshell, the policy allows any attorney or staff member to work reduced hours if he or she demonstrates a business case for reducing hours. A "business case" includes a description of the work proposed to be done, the schedule on which the work will be done, availability in emergencies, and the benefit to the firm of the new schedule. Attorneys and staff members who reduce their hours will receive a proportional reduction in pay, but will continue to advance professionally within the firm. This is different from our former part-time policy in several ways: reduced hours are not limited to attorneys who need them for childcare; associates who reduce hours will remain on the partnership track if they would remain on track if they had not reduced their hours; reduced hours are available to members and staff; and reduced schedules will be monitored to ensure that hours in excess of the scheduled hours are not routinely worked. A Balanced Hours Coordinator will oversee the program.

The purpose of the policy is to allow members and employees of our firm to reduce their hours, if they wish, thereby reducing attrition. Reducing attrition will save the firm a significant amount of money and will improve the firm's relationship with its clients, who appreciate stability in their representation. In addition, we anticipate that reduced attrition will enhance our firm culture, diminish stress for individuals, and improve our recruiting season. Additional information will be made available to you in the coming weeks regarding the importance of this policy to the firm's future success.

The Balanced Hours Policy is extremely important to our firm, and everyone is expected to work to implement it successfully. The policy will require certain changes in the way we operate, including the way cases are staffed and the way members and employees are evaluated. We will be holding meetings several times a week for the next few weeks to discuss these changes in detail. The schedule is as follows:

        February 24, noon: For Members Only
        February 25, noon: Open meeting for all
        February 26, 4:00 p.m.:   For attorneys only
        February 27, 8:30 a.m.:   For staff only
        February 28, noon: Open meeting for all
        March 3, 10:00 a.m.:   Open meeting for all

Every member and employee of the firm must attend at least one meeting.
If you cannot make one of the scheduled meetings, contact me right away.

The new Balanced Hours Policy is an important initiative for our firm. It is part of a larger vision for the firm's future that aims to ensure the firm's continued commitment to providing the highest quality legal services for our clients while at the same time providing a professionally rewarding environment for our attorneys. Everyone must cooperate in implementing this policy if we are to achieve success. If you have any questions or concerns, please address them immediately with me or another member of the Management Committee.

Appendix 2

Sample Questionnaire

Our firm is always looking to improve its performance, both as counsel to our clients and as an organization that provides a professionally rewarding and personally satisfying place to work. This questionnaire is being sent to you to help the firm identify its strengths and weaknesses as a place to work. It is very important that every attorney in the firm respond to this questionnaire, and also that all responses are accurate and complete. If we need to maintain or change our way of doing business, we won't know that unless we have everyone's honest input. Please be assured that no attempt will be made to match answers to individual attorneys; the firm is interested in aggregated information only. That said, you should always feel free to discuss your opinions of the firm with firm management.

Please respond to this questionnaire today. All responses are due by Friday and should be placed in a sealed envelope and dropped off in the box in ___. Thank you for taking the time to help us be the best we can be.

1. Are you a   __partner   __associate   __of counsel   or   __contract attorney?

2. How long have you been with the firm?
   __0-2 years   __3-5 years   __6-9 years   __10-14 years   __15 or more years

3. Are you   __male   __female?

4. Have you worked at other law firms as an attorney?   __yes   __no

5. Looking at the last three years, how many hours a year do you bill on average?
   __0-1000   __1001-1500   __1501-1800   __1801-2000   __2001-2200
   __2201-2400   __2401-2600   __more than 2600

6. Looking at the last three years, how many hours do you work on average in order to bill the hours stated in response to the previous question?
   __0-1000   __1001-1500   __1501-1800   __1801-2000   __2001-2200
   __2201-2400   __2401-2600   __2601-2800   __2801-3000
   __more than 3000

For the next series of questions, please circle the answer that indicates how much you agree with each statement below, using 5 to indicate strong agreement, 4 to indicate agreement, 3 to indicate neutrality, 2 to indicate disagreement, 1 to indicate strong disagreement, and 0 to indicate that the statement is not applicable to you.

7. The billable work I do at the firm is interesting.   5 4 3 2 1 0

8. I am improving my skills as a lawyer through my work assignments.   5 4 3 2 1 0

9. I am working on at least one case involving a client that is important to the firm or that is highly visible.   5 4 3 2 1 0

10. The attorney(s) who supervise my work give me support when I need it.   5 4 3 2 1 0

11. I get regular feedback about my work from my supervising attorney(s).   5 4 3 2 1 0

12. I have had a formal performance evaluation within the last year.   5 4 3 2 1 0

13. I believe I am on track to advance in my career at the firm.   5 4 3 2 1 0

14. I am doing at least 50 hours of pro bono work each year.   5 4 3 2 1 0

15. I take at least one CLE course each year.   5 4 3 2 1 0

16. I participate in national or local bar activities (not just membership).   5 4 3 2 1 0

17. I do some business development activity each week (speaking, writing, networking, etc.).   5 4 3 2 1 0

18. I would like to bill fewer hours each year.   5 4 3 2 1 0

19. I am satisfied with the total number of hours I am working overall.   5 4 3 2 1 0

20. My workload is too heavy.   5 4 3 2 1 0

21. I have a mentor in the firm.   5 4 3 2 1 0

22. I have role models in the firm.   5 4 3 2 1 0

23. I am satisfied with the amount of compensation I receive.   5 4 3 2 1 0

24. I find working at the firm to be professionally rewarding.   5 4 3 2 1 0

25. I am happy working at the firm.   5 4 3 2 1 0

26. I am considering leaving the firm within the next two years.   5 4 3 2 1 0

27. I am actively looking for another job right now.   5 4 3 2 1 0

For the next set of questions, please provide written answers. Feel free to type your answers if you wish and submit them on a separate piece of paper, indicating the question to which you are responding.

28. How able do you feel to balance your work responsibilities and your personal responsibilities or interests?

29. If you could change anything you want about your job (e.g., hours, pay, type of work, supervision, environment), what would you change?

30. If you were not able to make the changes stated in your answer to the previous question, would you continue to work at the firm? How?

31. Do you want to work an alternative schedule (e.g., reduced hours, telecommuting)? Why or why not?

32. What do you perceive are the causes of attrition at our firm?

33. If you were running the firm, what changes would you make to improve the firm?

34. Is there anything else you would like to say about the firm or your work experience here?

Appendix 3

Attrition Cost Worksheet[1]

While industry estimates are that it costs 200% of a professional's salary to replace him or her, the actual costs related to attrition and replacement necessarily vary by firm. This worksheet is an example of the items firms might consider in calculating actual attrition and replacement costs; each firm should customize the worksheet to reflect its business and values.

This worksheet is designed to estimate the costs of attrition for the prior year. The first section asks for demographic information. The second section calculates the individual and administrative costs incurred when an attorney leaves, and the third section calculates the individual and administrative costs of new hires. The fourth section captures training costs, and the fifth section includes extraordinary expenses not covered in the other sections. The final section totals the costs for the year.

■ Part I: Demographics

1. State the number of attorneys in each of the following categories who left the firm in the last calendar year:

    Equity Partners _____

    Non-equity Partners _____

    Of counsel _____

    Associates _____

    Total _____

2. Show the demographic composition of the class of departing attorneys:

    Number of males: ____

    Number of females: ____

    Number of white attorneys: _____

    Number of minority attorneys: ____

    Number of part-time attorneys: _____

---

[1] © 2003 Cynthia Thomas Calvert

3. State the length of time the departed attorneys were with the firm (i.e., if two first-year associates left, put a "2" after "0-2 years"):

   0-2 years_____   3-5 years_____   6-8 years_____   8-10 years_____
   Over 10 years_____

4. How many of the departing attorneys were asked to leave by the firm? _____

   What percentage of the departures were voluntary on the part of the attorneys? _____%

5. State the number of new hires the firm made in each of the following categories:

   Replacement of departed attorneys: _____

   New hires that were part of the firm's planned growth: _____

   Total new hires: _____

   Percentage of new hires who replaced departed attorneys: _____%

■ Part II: Departure-Related Costs

A. Individual Costs

Provide the following information for *each* departed attorney who left the firm voluntarily.

6. Calculate the billable hours revenue lost between the time of resignation and the time a replacement attorney was hired. To calculate this figure, determine the attorney's average weekly billable hours, multiply by the attorney's billing rate, and multiply the average by the number of weeks the attorney's position was vacant. If some or all of the attorney's work was shifted to other attorneys, estimate the percentage of work shifted and reduce the first calculation by this percent. *Note: human resources professionals estimate that 40% of a professional's work is not reassigned when he or she departs. If you are uncertain of how much of the work was shifted, you may want to multiply the lost billable hours revenue by 40% as an estimate.* Avg. weekly billable hours _____ x billing rate _____ x No. weeks position vacant _____ x Reduced by work shifted .40 =	$_____

7. For each departed attorney, list the clients each took with him or her. Estimate the value of each lost client to the firm, using past or anticipated billings. *Note: if the clients were longstanding clients, you may need to include several years of billings to accurately reflect the loss.*	$_____
8. If the departed attorney was employed by the firm for less than five years, calculate the total direct costs incurred by the firm to hire the attorney (flyback expenses, meals and entertainment, moving expenses, hiring bonuses, clerkship bonuses, bar expenses, etc.). *Note: for an attorney who has been employed for more than three years, you may want to reduce the direct costs if you believe the firm got some benefit during the time the attorney was employed as a result of the incurred costs.*	$_____
9. If the departed attorney was employed by the firm for less than five years, calculate the costs incurred to train the attorney who departed (continuing education expenses, proportional costs of in-house training, other tuition). If your firm writes off hours of attorneys who are new to the practice of law or who spend time getting up to speed on client matters, include the amounts written off for this attorney. *Note: for an attorney who has been employed for more than three years, you may want to reduce the direct costs if you believe the firm got some benefit during the time the attorney was employed as a result of the incurred costs.*	$_____
10. Other direct costs. If the firm held a farewell event, issued announcements related to the departure, paid severance, continued insurance payments, provided outplacement services, or incurred any other direct costs associated with the *voluntarily* departed attorney, include them here.	$_____

11. Calculate the savings realized as a result of the departure between the time of resignation and the time a replacement attorney was hired. Determine the cost to the firm of the attorney's salary plus benefits for the period of time the attorney's position was vacant. Do not include the cost of fixed overhead (e.g., rent, utilities) because the firm continues to bear those costs while the position is vacant. If the firm saves money on overhead related to the attorney (e.g., malpractice insurance), that can be deducted for the period of time the position is vacant.
    Weekly salary plus benefits _____
                     x
    Number of weeks position vacant _____
                     +
    Savings on attorney-related overhead _____ =
	($_____)

12. Net cost to firm as a result of attorney's departure. *Subtract the amount in line 11 from the total of lines 6, 7, 8, 9, and 10.*	$_____
13. Total net departure costs for prior year (add all the line 11s for the departed attorneys).	$_____

B. Administrative and Indirect Costs

Provide the following information for the firm's administrative functions.

14. Identify the administrative personnel involved in terminating employees. These may include the firm administrator, human resources staff, payroll department, benefits coordinator, administrative support (secretarial and paralegal) supervisors, and marketing staff (deletions to firm's professional directory listings, changes to letterhead, etc.). For each individual, estimate the amount of time each spends annually on termination-related tasks and multiply that percent by the individual's salary, benefits, and bonus package. Add the total for each individual and include the total here.	$ _____
15. Estimate the cost of administrative partner hours related to attrition. Include time spent by supervising attorneys and/or department heads: in group meetings to discuss attrition generally and particular attorney departures; in one-on-one meetings with the departing attorneys; in meetings with remaining attorneys to reassign work; to communicate with clients; to attend farewell events; and to coordinate with firm administrators to initiate the process of hiring a replacement attorney. Multiply the estimated number of hours by the partners' hourly billable rate and total for each departed attorney.	$ _____
16. Multiply the total of lines 14 and 15 by the percentage of departures that were voluntary (*from line 4 above*) for the total annual administrative and indirect costs related to departures:	$ _____

Part III. Replacement Hire Costs

A. Individual Costs

Provide the following information for *each* new attorney who was hired to replace a departed attorney.

17. Calculate the direct costs incurred in the hiring. These include flyback travel expenses, recruiting entertainment expenses, signing or hiring bonuses, clerkship bonuses, moving expenses, bar expenses, fees paid to headhunters, and referral fees paid to others.	$ _____
18. If the salary paid to the new attorney is higher than the salary paid to the departed attorney, or if additional benefits are provided to the new attorney at cost above the cost of benefits for the departed attorney, include that here.	$ _____
19. Add the total individual direct costs for each new hire and put the total here.	$ _____

B. Administrative and Indirect Costs

Provide the following information for the firm's administrative functions.

20. Identify the administrative personnel involved in recruiting and hiring employees. These may include the firm administrator, human resources staff, payroll department, benefits coordinator, administrative support (secretarial and paralegal) supervisors, and marketing staff (additions to firm's professional directory listings, changes to letterhead, announcements, etc.). For each individual, estimate the amount of time each spends annually on hiring-related tasks and multiply that percent by the individual's salary, benefits, and bonus package. Add the total for each individual and include the total here.	$ _____
21. Calculate the total spent advertising job openings.	$ _____
22. Calculate the costs of sending firm's attorneys to on-campus interviews (include both direct expenses such as travel costs and indirect expenses such as lost billable time).	$ _____
23. Calculate the value of the billable hours spent by the firm's hiring committee (multiply the time spent by each attorney on the committee by the attorney's billable rate and calculate total for all).	$ _____
24. Calculate the value of the billable hours spent by the firm's attorneys to interview candidates for job openings (multiply the time spent by each attorney by the attorney's billable rate and calculate total for all).	$ _____
25. Multiply the total of lines 20, 21, 22, 23, and 24 by the percentage of the new hires that replaced departed attorneys (from line 5 above) for the total administrative and indirect costs related to new hires.	$ _____

■ Part IV: Training Costs

A. Individual Costs

Provide information for each new hire who replaced a departed attorney.

26. Direct costs of training. Include such costs as bar exam review courses, CLE courses, and professionalism courses, and any travel costs related to attendance at the training.	$ _____
27. Hours written off client bills while the attorney gets up to speed. Also include reductions in the hourly billable rate that are made to reflect the attorney's relative lack of experience or skill.	$ _____

28. Calculate the value of the time used by the new attorney to get oriented and participate in training.	$ _____
29. Calculate the value of the time spent by supervising attorneys to get the new attorney up to speed.	$ _____
30. Total the costs on lines 26, 27, 28, and 29 for each new hire and put the total here.	$ _____

B. Administrative and Indirect Training Costs

31. Identify the administrative personnel involved in orienting and training new attorneys. These may include the firm administrator, human resources staff, administrative support (secretarial and paralegal) supervisors, and marketing staff (business development). For each individual, estimate the amount of time each spends annually on training-related tasks and multiply that percent by the individual's salary, benefits, and bonus package. Add the total for each individual and include the total here.	$ _____
32. Calculate the cost of firm-provided training programs.	$ _____
33. Multiply the total of lines 31 and 32 by the percentage of the new hires who replaced departed attorneys (from line 5 above) for the total administrative and indirect costs related to training of new attorneys.	$ _____

■ Part V: Extraordinary Costs

If your firm incurred extraordinary costs related to its attrition or recruiting in the past year, include them in this section.

34. Extraordinary costs not captured above such as the hiring of a public relations firm to repair damage to the firm's image caused by high attrition or to improve the firm's image to enhance its recruiting efforts; the loss of clients due to high attrition, as opposed to the loss of any particular attorney; or the hiring of temporary attorneys or contract attorneys to do work that would have been done by departed attorneys.	$ _____

■ Part VI: Total Attrition Costs

35. Total lines 13, 16, 19, 25, 30, 33, and 34, above. This is your total attrition-related cost for the prior year.	$ _____

It is important to note that these attrition costs are only the *tangible* costs. Intangible costs of attrition include: lost knowledge, skills, and contacts; reduced employee morale; increased stress for attorneys who remain at the firm; client dissatisfaction; decreased productivity due to loss of synergy and to the distraction caused by the departures; and damage to the firm's reputation.

Appendix 4

Balanced Hours Schedule Checklist for Attorneys

Pre-Plan for a Balanced Hours Schedule

- [ ] Consider the type of schedule needed to meet your obligations outside of the office (fewer hours per day, per week, annually, etc.). If more than one schedule would work for you, prioritize your options.

- [ ] Consider the type of schedule best suited to your type of practice and your clients, and think about a schedule that will accommodate your needs and the firm's needs.

- [ ] Decide if the new schedule is needed indefinitely, or if there is a foreseeable ending point.

- [ ] Decide if the new schedule is needed immediately, or when it should start.

- [ ] List the nonbillable work that needs to be done during your hours in the office (administrative, business development, professional development, etc.) and the amount of time needed for this nonbillable work.

- [ ] State the number of billable hours you can work per week/month/year, and calculate the number as a percentage of a full-time schedule.

- [ ] Consider how your work will be done on a balanced hours schedule. Will you need to give up some cases or duties, have more assistance from paralegals or junior associates, or automate some tasks?

- [ ] Consider how you will handle emergencies at work. How can you work extra hours if necessary?

- [ ] Consider how you will handle emergencies outside of work. What types of emergencies are likely to arise, and how can you handle them if they arise during your normal working hours?

☐ Discuss your ideas for a balanced hours schedule with someone in your firm who has worked balanced hours. If no one is available, seek someone with experience outside your firm. Find out what has worked well and what the person would have done differently.

Create a Proposal

☐ Create a written proposal that includes the following elements:

____ The schedule you want to work.

____ How the proposed schedule will meet the needs of the firm and clients.

____ The work that will have to be reassigned, delegated, or done differently.

____ If your firm's policy does not spell it out, include how your balanced hours schedule will affect compensation, bonuses, benefits, advancement, and business development expectations.

____ If your firm's policy does not spell it out, include how you will be compensated if you work more hours than you are scheduled to, including comp time.

____ The technology (laptop, fax machine, etc.) and tech support you will need.

____ The nonbillable work you will do and when.

____ What clients will be told about your balanced hours schedule.

____ The duration of the balanced schedule, if an ending point is contemplated.

____ Availability for emergencies in the office.

____ Accessibility when outside the office.

____ Schedule for reviewing the effectiveness of the balanced hours schedule.

☐ Sit down with your supervising attorney to discuss the proposal.

☐ After making any necessary revisions, submit your proposal pursuant to the firm's policy to the designated decision maker.

Implement the Schedule

- ☐ Discuss your new schedule with your administrative and legal support personnel. Make sure they know when they can expect to see you in the office, how they can reach you outside of the office, and what clients and others are to be told about where you are when you aren't in the office.

- ☐ Schedule social events such as lunches with other attorneys in your firm to maintain your visibility.

- ☐ Be very prompt in responding to phone messages and e-mails so others do not sense you are unavailable.

- ☐ Discuss your new schedule with clients as you and your supervisors have determined appropriate. Make sure they have alternative ways of reaching you or the name of another attorney to contact if you are not in the office.

- ☐ If you find yourself with too much work, discuss it with your supervisor or the firm's Balanced Hours Coordinator rather than suffering silently or falling behind.

Appendix 5

Model Balanced Hours Policy[1]

■ Introduction

Our Firm's strength is derived from is its diverse and deeply talented group of attorneys. As a firm, we are committed to maintaining and promoting our diversity and talent. A key way for us to demonstrate our commitment is to recognize that our attorneys have responsibilities and interests outside the Firm that need to be supported and that these responsibilities and interests will affect our attorneys' work schedules.

Balanced hours schedules are available to our attorneys as one way of supporting their lives outside the office. (Similar schedules are available for staff, as set out in the staff manual.) Balanced hours schedules are individually tailored reduced hours schedules designed to meet the needs of the attorney and the needs of the Firm and its clients. Requests for balanced hours schedules will be considered in light of the business needs of the Firm and the Firm's clients, and will be granted whenever possible. The Firm believes that balanced hours schedules should not affect an attorney's professional development or ability to provide professional service to the Firm, clients, the bar, and the community.

This policy sets forth the procedure for proposing a balanced hours schedule, and the general guidelines applicable to balanced hours schedules. Questions about the policy or its application should be directed to the Balanced Hours Coordinator.

■ Expectations

The Firm expects all of its attorneys to provide professional and prompt service to clients. It also expects all of its attorneys to provide pro bono services in accordance with the Firm's policy, to continue their legal education, to engage in business development, to participate in bar activities, and to share in Firm administrative and managerial duties. Balanced hours attorneys should anticipate and meet these expectations.

---

[1] © 2001 Joan Williams and Cynthia Thomas Calvert

■ Flexibility

Meeting client needs often requires flexibility in scheduling, and all attorneys are expected to be flexible in their scheduling when necessary. The Firm will not expect balanced hours attorneys to work in their off-hours on a regular basis, but it may be necessary from time to time for a balanced hours attorney to come into the office or work from another location when not scheduled to do so. When this happens, every effort will be made to provide the attorney compensatory time off within the same pay period as the non-scheduled work. If it is not possible for the attorney to take compensatory time off, the attorney will be compensated in accordance with the compensation guidelines of this policy.

■ Availability and Duration

Balanced hours schedules are available to all attorneys, assuming an acceptable proposal is made. There is no minimum length of time that an attorney must work full-time before a balanced hours request will be considered. The Firm recognizes that attorneys' schedules will change over time, and understands that balanced hours attorneys may wish to return to standard hours schedules or to stay on balanced hours indefinitely. Changes will be accommodated, again assuming an acceptable proposal is made. There is no minimum or maximum length of time an attorney may work a balanced hours schedule.

■ Schedules

Balanced hours schedules are to be tailored to meet the individual needs of attorneys. The schedules may include fewer hours per week, per month, or per year. (The Firm finds that beneficial continuity of service to clients generally requires attorneys to work at least 50% of a standard hours schedule, but proposals to work less than 50% will be considered.)

The schedules should be described in terms of percentage of a standard hours schedule, which for these purposes is defined as [1,800] billable hours and [400] nonbillable hours. [Note: for firms without billable or other hourly requirements, the standard schedule can be determined by averaging the attorney's own work hours over a several year period or over his or her entire career with the firm.] Balanced hours schedules are to include both billable and nonbillable time in proportion to the billable and nonbillable hours the attorneys worked when on standard schedules. (For new hires, the Balanced Hours Coordinator will suggest a ratio based on a typical attorney's experience at the Firm.)

■ Balanced Hours Proposals

An attorney wishing to work a balanced hours schedule should first explore the types of balanced hours schedules worked by other attorneys in the Firm and elsewhere, and determine what type of schedule would best suit his or her individual needs. Information about balanced hours schedules is kept by the Balanced Hours Coordinator and is available on the Firm's intranet. The attorney should work with the Balanced Hours Coordinator to complete the pre-proposal questionnaire, which covers topics such as how the attorney will accomplish his or her work and how the attorney will be available for emergencies, and then draft the proposal. Draft proposals should be reviewed by the Balanced Hours Coordinator and submitted to the attorney's supervising attorney(s) and practice head. The supervising attorney(s) and practice head will be asked to consider various factors relating to how work will be performed under the proposed balanced hours schedule. The Firm anticipates that if the supervising attorney(s) and/or practice head have objections to the proposal, they will discuss the objections and suggest revisions to the attorney. The practice head will forward it, with his or her recommendation as to approval, to the Management Committee for final consideration.

■ Compensation

Associates and counsel working balanced hours schedules will be compensated proportionally to standard hours attorneys of their same class year. For example, an associate working 80% of a standard hours schedule will earn 80% of the standard hours salary for an associate in her same class. (Associates and counsel working less than 50% of a standard schedule may be compensated on an hourly basis if the Balanced Hours Coordinator and their practice heads determine that hourly compensation is more feasible.)

Partners will be compensated in accordance with the recommendations of the Compensation Committee, which will determine the partner share of a balanced hours attorney as if the attorney were working a standard schedule and then adjust the share amount to reflect the proportion of hours worked. Compensation based on business origination credits will be paid at full rates and not adjusted proportionally.

Balanced hours attorneys remain eligible for bonuses, which will be awarded in proportion with the attorneys' schedules. For bonuses based on the number of hours over target worked, balanced hours attorneys will receive bonuses based on the number of hours over their balanced hours schedule worked.

■ Benefits

Balanced hours attorneys remain eligible for the same benefits as standard hours attorneys [except that attorneys working less than 50% or less than 25 hours per week are ineligible for medical, dental, life, and disability insurance as stated in the Firm's policies]. [Balanced hours attorneys are eligible for the same benefits as standard hours attorneys, pro-rated to reflect the proportion of a standard schedule the balanced hours attorney is working. For example, if a balanced hours attorney works 80% of a standard schedule, the firm will pay 80% of the premium for his or her health, dental, life, and disability insurance and the balanced hours attorney will be responsible for the remainder of the premium.]

■ Technology

The Firm provides all attorneys with an annual stipend for use in purchasing work-related technology. The stipend may be used for such things as cellular telephones and service, Blackberries, fax machines, second phone lines, and computers. Balanced hours attorneys are urged to consider their needs for communicating with the office and with clients when deciding how to use their stipend. At a minimum, a fax machine and cellular telephone should be purchased. If additional stipend amounts are needed, the Firm will consider advancing the additional amounts against the next year's stipend.

■ Assignments

Balanced hours attorneys will receive the same types of assignments as standard hours attorneys, adjusted to take work hours into account. Balanced hours attorneys will not receive a disproportionate amount of routine work. The Balanced Hours Coordinator will review the type of work done by balanced hours attorneys to ensure compliance with this guideline.

■ Partnership Track

The Firm evaluates its associates and counsel regularly to ensure they are performing at a level that makes them eligible for partnership. Factors considered include, but are not limited to, quality of work, quality of relationships with clients and colleagues, skill development, and ability to attract new business. Working a balanced hours schedule does not change the evaluation process or the factors considered, and balanced hours associates and counsel remain eligible for partnership. Working a balanced hours schedule may extend the time at which an attorney is considered for partnership, depending on the proportion of standard hours worked and the duration of the balanced hours schedule. For example, an associate who works a standard schedule for six years and an 80% of standard schedule for two years is likely to be considered with other associates of his class, but an associate who works a 60% schedule for six years will likely find his partnership track extended by two or more years.

■ Periodic Reviews

The success of each balanced hours schedule will be reviewed with the attorney, Balanced Hours Coordinator, and the attorney's supervisor(s) every three [six] months. If changes to the schedule are necessary, they will be made in writing. In addition to the six-month reviews, the attorney and his or her supervisor(s) are encouraged to communicate with each other and/or the Balanced Hours Coordinator on an ongoing basis about issues that arise regarding the schedule. The Balanced Hours Coordinator will review the hours worked by balanced hours attorneys and will address consistent excessive hours with the attorney and the attorney's supervisor(s) on an ongoing basis.

■ About the Authors

Joan Williams, prize-winning author and Professor of Law at American University, Washington College of Law, is the Director of WorkLife Law and Co-Director of the Project on Attorney Retention (PAR). The author of *Unbending Gender: Why Work and Family Conflict and What To Do About It* (Oxford University Press, 1999), she was awarded the Gustavus Myers Outstanding Book Award. She has been widely quoted in the press, in publications as diverse as *The Wall Street Journal, Business Week*, *The New York Times, The Washington Post, Parenting Magazine, Working Mother*, and *O*, and has appeared in other media, including CBS Nightly News, CSPAN, *The Diane Rehm Show, Public Interest,* and *Talk of the Nation.* She was featured on the PBS documentary *Juggling Work and Family*, with Hedrick Smith. The author of one of the most cited law review articles ever written, and roughly 50 other law review articles, she has had articles excerpted in casebooks for six different subjects. She has taught at Harvard, University of Virginia, and UC Hastings law schools, and has lectured widely, including at Yale, Harvard, Columbia, Pennsylvania, Cornell, Duke, and more than a dozen other law schools, and in Chile, Ecuador, Guatemala, and Peru.

Cynthia Thomas Calvert is a co-director of the Project for Attorney Retention and deputy director of the Program on WorkLife Law. She advises law firms and attorneys about effective part-time programs, and frequently speaks and writes about work/life issues. Ms. Calvert is also a practicing attorney in the District of Columbia and Maryland. She has worked full-time, part-time, and flex-time as both a partner and an associate at D.C.'s Miller, Cassidy, Larroca & Lewin, L.L.P. (now part of Baker Botts LLP). She has been involved with issues concerning alternative work arrangements for more than fourteen years, including work done in connection with the Women's Bar Association of the District of Columbia. She now has her own employment law practice, counseling businesses on compliance issues and prevention of employee lawsuits. Ms. Calvert received her J.D. from the Georgetown University Law Center, *cum laude*, in 1985 and clerked for the Honorable Thomas Penfield Jackson (D.D.C.). She is married and has two children.

For more information about the **Project for Attorney Retention** and **WorkLife Law**, please visit **www.pardc.org** and **www.worklifelaw.org**.

■ About NALP

Founded in 1971 as the National Association for Law Placement, Inc.® NALP is a nonprofit education association with a membership including virtually every ABA-accredited law school and nearly 1,000 legal employers. NALP's member representatives number more than 1,700 and include legal recruitment and professional development administrators from law firms, government agencies, corporations, and public interest organizations as well as career services professionals from law schools.

To learn more about NALP — and about additional resources available from NALP — visit **www.nalp.org**. NALP also offers two additional web sites:

- For an online directory of legal employers and information on their hiring criteria, visit **www. nalpdirectory.com**.

- For information on public service opportunities for law students and lawyers, visit the site of NALP's Public Service Law Network Worldwide (PSLawNet) at **www.pslawnet.org**.

In addition, information on research conducted by The NALP Foundation for Law Career Research and Education can be found at **www.nalpfoundation.org**.